A Vision Quest

A Vision Quest

John S. Dunne

University of Notre Dame Press

Notre Dame, Indiana

Copyright © 2006 by University of Notre Dame
Notre Dame, Indiana 46556
www.undpress.nd.edu
All Rights Reserved
Published in the United States of America

Library of Congress Cataloging in-Publication Data

Dunne, John S., 1929–
A vision quest / John S. Dunne.
p.   cm.
Includes bibliographical references and index.
ISBN 0-268-02584-3 (pbk. : alk. paper)
1. Spirituality.   I. Title.
BL624.D8375   2006
248—dc22
2005034405

Contents

Preface

◆ "If we had a keen vision and feeling of all ordinary human life," George Eliot says in *Middlemarch*, "it would be like hearing the grass grow or the squirrel's heart beat, and we should die of that roar which lies on the other side of silence."[1] Words are on one side of silence, and music is on the other side of silence, and in the silence between words and music vision may be found.

I call this book *A Vision Quest*, borrowing the term from native American tradition where the youth, coming of age, keeps a solitary vigil, seeking spiritual power and knowledge of the identity of his guardian spirit through a vision. What I am seeking is something similar out of the silence between words and music. The modern vision of the world is one of evolution, matter and life and intelligence, where as Teilhard de Chardin says "Everything that rises must converge."[2] The ancient vision was one of emanation, everything cascading down from the One, intelligence and life and matter. I imagine bringing the two visions together here into one of a great circle, everything coming from God and returning to God, where, as the old Bedouin said to Lawrence of Arabia, "The love is from God and of God and towards God."[3]

"We can know more than we can tell,"[4] as Michael Polanyi says, and so there is a tacit dimension in knowing, an element of silence. We can tell our story, but there is something we can know and cannot quite tell, we can know our relationship, the *I and thou* in which we live, and vision arises out of the relationship, so that the *I* of a life depends for its meaning on the *thou* of the life. There is what we can tell of this in words, the story, and there is what we can express in music, the song, and in between there is this tacit knowing of the relationship, the silence. Words and music come together in song, and "song is the leap of mind in the eternal breaking out into sound,"[5] as Saint Thomas Aquinas says, and so the silence that is broken by song, at least by sacred song, is the silence of an eternal vision of *I and thou* with God, a vision of the great circle of coming from God and returning to God. Yet what of secular song? The great circle of vision passes through the world, through "being there" in the world and *I and thou* with human beings, and secular song too is a "leap of mind in the eternal breaking out into sound."

If words then are on one side of silence and music is on the other side of silence, what is "that roar which lies on the other side of silence"? Well, if we did hear the grass grow and the squirrel's heart beat and all such sounds it would be a roar on the other side of what is now silence. It would be a roar unless it were a harmony. Actually we do hear the wind and the rain and the thunder, we hear the sound of the surf, we hear the song of the birds and the crickets. "What we call music in our everyday language is only a miniature," Inayat Khan says, "which our intelligence has grasped from that music or harmony of the whole universe which is working behind everything, and which is the source and origin of nature."[6] We listen to this when we listen to music and when we listen to the silence, dwelling in what we can know and cannot tell.

Words and music are the tracks of human evolution, I find, words belonging to the left brain and the right hand, music to the right brain and the left hand. Yet the human brain is not the human mind, I want to say, but situates the mind, and matter generally situates as well as being situated in space and time. What is more, the world's first languages were in song, I want to say with Vico, and the separation and separate development of words and music go with the separation and separate development of human beings and point on to an ultimate reunion with humanity and with God in a vision of everything coming from God and everything returning to God on the mystic road of love.

I end with a song and dance cycle, also called "A Vision Quest" like the book itself. This book I am writing after my memoir, *A Journey with God in Time,* and if my memoir corresponds to Saint Augustine telling his life story in *Confessions* books 1–9, this book corresponds to his vision quest in *Confessions* books 10–13 on memory and time and the beginning of time. Saint Augustine seems to have had a writer's block of some kind as his earlier books were mostly left unfinished, but in the *Confessions* he found his voice and his vision and all his great works follow. Well, here I am at the end just getting to where he began. Or then again maybe I am doing it all backwards, starting in my first book, *The City of the Gods,* where he ended in *The City of God.* At any rate, he has clearly been for me a principal source of inspiration.

A Vision Quest

We are too late for the gods and too early for Being.
—Martin Heidegger

◆ When we feel the wonder of existence, looking up at the stars on a summer night, the wonder that all these things are, these worlds that appear as points of light in the night sky, we know "we are too late for the gods," as Martin Heidegger says, "and too early for Being."[1] Knowing these points of light are worlds, we know we are too late for the gods. Feeling the wonder, nevertheless, we know we are too early for Being, too early to know how all beings are of Being, by emanation or by evolution. Those are the two common visions, the ancient vision of emanation of all from the One and the modern vision of evolution of all towards the One.

A vision quest, as it is called among the American Indians, is a solitary vigil of a youth seeking spiritual power and seeking to know the identity of his guardian spirit. If I may go on such a quest, who am not an American Indian and no longer a youth, I too will be seeking spiritual power and seeking to know the identity of the God who is my companion on the journey of my life. I have long believed my life is a journey in time and God is my companion on the way. The spiritual power I am seeking is like that of the elven rings in Tolkien's trilogy, "they were not made as weapons of war or conquest: that was not their power. Those who made them did not desire strength or domination or hoarded wealth, but understanding, making, and healing, to preserve all things unstained."[2] And the identity of the God who is my companion is the God I have always believed in, the God-with-us of the Gospels, as for Merlin "the god, who was God."[3] What, though, is the vision?

I want to think that the ancient vision of emanation of all from the One and the modern vision of evolution of all towards the One can come together in something like a great circle of life and light and love. It would be like the vision implicit in the words of the old Bedouin to Lawrence of Arabia, "The love is from God and of God and towards God."[4] I came upon the ancient vision of emanation when I was working on my doctoral dissertation on Saint Thomas and his theology of participation. I learned of the Platonic or Neoplatonic elements in his thought, the One, the emanation of all from the One, and the return of all to the One. Then when I began teaching I came upon the modern vision of evolution in the thought of Teilhard de Chardin, how "everything that rises must converge." I see a parallel between the descending stages of emanation, mind, soul, and body, and the ascending stages of evolution, matter, life, and intelligence.

I can see a parallel also between the return (*epistrophe*) of all to the One and the evolution of all towards the One. Creation was a problem in the ancient vision of emanation as well as in the modern vision of evolution. The solution of Saint Thomas was to see creation as a relation rather than a process, and that works as well with evolution as with emanation. I see redemption, too, as a relation, us entering into the relation of Jesus with his God. Let us see what bearing the relation may have on the process.

"We are too late for the gods." It is the idea of creation, I suppose, and of one God, that makes us too late for the gods. "It is not *how* things are in the world that is mystical, but *that* it exists,"[5] Wittgenstein says. The wonder of existence, "*that* it exists," is the wonder of Being. The gods are related rather to "*how* things are in the world," and that too is a wonder for us, especially in childhood. There is a story, *The Watchful Gods,* by Van Tilburg Clark, where "All things are full of gods,"[6] as Thales said, for a child's wonder, but become empty of gods as the child grows up. If we were to sustain a child's wonder in later life, the world could still be full of gods for us. I suppose the meaning of Thales' saying, "All things are full of gods," is that the world is animate, alive. To relate to it as a live world is very different from relating to it as an inanimate world.

When I studied Saint Thomas Aquinas, I noticed that his world was inanimate whereas the world of Aristotle, whose philosophy he was using, was an animate world, a live world. I suppose this was a result of going from the gods to God, the transcendence of God leaving the world empty of gods, though Aquinas believed in the angels, thinking of them as pure spirits rather than as souls of the world. I have always wondered if modern science comes of considering the world empty of gods and if science therefore arises from the idea of the transcendence of God. Certainly there was an ancient science and there were scientific thinkers like Archimedes whose science was compatible with a world full of gods.

Now evolutionary and molecular biology, the leading edge of science in our time, for instance in the human genome project, has brought scientific thinking in its fully developed and mathematical form to bear upon life and living beings. It may be, though, that new forms of mathematics are needed to deal with life and with intelligence. Even to deal with matter itself it has been necessary to introduce an element of uncertainty into calculations. It may be necessary to generalize the principle of uncertainty in order to deal with life and with intelligence. Wherever we find the element of chance, it seems, in the interactions of matter, in the evolution of life, in human affairs and interactions, we have the element of our unknowing. Chance, I want to think, is a name for our unknowing.

So to say "we are too late for the gods" is to speak of our unknowing, like "the cloud of unknowing in the which a soul is oned with God."[7] It is a conscious unknowing, a knowing unknowing, and that is how "a soul is oned with God." Actually there is a twofold relation here, one of knowing and one of loving. There is a knowing unknowing and there is a loving, "into the darkness with love."[8] Knowing is taking things in; loving is going out to things. We find God in our unknowing, and we go out to meet God there in the unknown.

We are "too early for Being," finding God in the play of chance, when in fact, as Einstein used to say, "God does not play dice." The transcendence of God goes somehow with the wonder of existence, "It is not *how* things are in the world that is mystical, but *that* it exists." If we find God in the play of chance, it is not as a hidden variable that eliminates the play of chance but rather as a transcendent cause that leaves chance intact. So in the interactions of matter, in the evolution of life, in human affairs and interactions, God does not intervene to create a hidden determinism, but leaves chance and our freedom intact. What we come upon in our unknowing is the wonder that is the mystical. We encounter Being, the wonder of existence and transcendence, in the chance encounters of beings.

"Subtle is the Lord God, but not malicious,"[9] Einstein said, and that first phrase became the title of his biography by Abraham Pais, *Subtle is the Lord.* Einstein would certainly have agreed with what I am saying, that chance is a name for our unknowing, but his view was one of determinism and his God was Spinoza's of immanence rather than of transcendence. I want to say too, "Subtle is the Lord God but not malicious," but the subtlety, as I understand it, is that of transcendence, that God is above and beyond the finite categories of our knowing. God is "too subtle," Saint Thomas More says in Robert Bolt's play *A Man for All Seasons.* "I don't know where he is or what he wants."[10] I too want to suggest an unknowing in saying "God is subtle," but it is an unknowing as in "the cloud of unknowing in the which a soul is oned with God" and in the motto "into the darkness with love."

Our unknowing, it is true, can be separated from our loving and can result then in a very negative vision. "What a book a devil's chaplain might write," Darwin says in a letter, "on the clumsy, wasteful, blundering, low, and horridly cruel works of nature!"[11] When we go "into the darkness" of our unknowing "with love," we come to a vision like that of Genesis, "And God saw that it was good."[12] To say it is good, or to say as Aquinas does, "all being is good" (*omne ens est bonum*),[13] is to perceive the wonder of existence, "the mystical," "not *how* things are in the world but *that* it exists." If knowing is taking things in and loving is going out to things, there is a knowing that comes of loving, a taking in that comes of going out, and that knowing is the perceiving of the wonder of existence, something that is usually concealed by being taken for granted.

I remember being a student in a course taught by Josef Pieper at Notre Dame around 1950 in which he discussed simply the question "What is philosophy?" and "all being is true" (*omne ens est verum*) and "all being is good" (*omne ens est bonum*). I had the feeling of being in the presence of a man of vision, and it seemed I was coming to share a vision that was at once simple and profound, a vision of the truth and goodness of all things. He spoke, I remember, also of the holocaust in Nazi Germany in the 1940s and of what inkling he had of it when it was going on. To say "all being is good" in the face of enormous evil in human affairs is indeed a paradox, and I suppose it is again the wonder of existence, "It is not *how* things are in the world that is mystical, but *that* it exists."

"God is vulnerable,"[14] that is what I heard in another class at that time, taught by another great follower of Saint Thomas, Jacques Maritain. If I connect God with "the mystical," with the wonder of existence, then I see God as vulnerable to "*how* things are in the world." There is love of God in that saying, "God is vulnerable," seeing God as all good up against evil in the world. In the vision of emanation there is evil as things get further and further from their origin in the One, cascading down from pure goodness, evil simply as lack of goodness. In the vision of evolution there is evil in that the good is under construction and is not yet finished, like the face of the child Mary Ann described by Flannery O'Connor, a face partially devastated by cancer, "grotesque but full of promise."[15]

Evil, I want to say, is "the mystery of iniquity," as in the King James Version of 2 Thessalonians 2:7, or "the mystery of lawlessness" in the Revised Standard Version, and if the law of God is essentially the law of love, to love God with all your heart and soul and to love your neighbor as yourself, evil is also the mystery of lovelessness. Thus at the bottom of Dante's Inferno there is ice. To speak of evil simply as the lack of goodness, or to speak of the good as something under construction is indeed to speak of good rather than evil. In itself evil is a mystery to us, a shadow cast by the light. "Subtle is the Lord God but not malicious," Einstein's saying, casts a shadow too. "Nature hides her secret because of her essential loftiness," he explains, "but not by means of ruse."[16] His vision of nature is very different from Darwin's, but he is thinking of the interactions of matter and Darwin of the struggle for survival.

There is a darker shadow in those words of Darwin, "What a book a devil's chaplain might write on the clumsy, wasteful, blundering, low, and horridly cruel works of nature!" I think of Tennessee Williams' play, *Suddenly Last Summer*, where there is a description of sea turtles being hatched on land and racing to the sea to escape the birds of prey who seek to devour them, and the character Sebastian saying "Well, now I've seen Him!"[17] meaning God. For me you see God when you perceive the wonder of existence. It is not *how* the sea turtles are hatched on land and race to the sea to escape the birds of prey that is mystical but *that* the world of sea turtles and birds of prey exists. God is vulnerable, as in this play Sebastian is vulnerable, to "*how* things are."

There is the darkest shadow of all, though, in the human affairs and interactions, as in the fate of Sebastian, who is partly devoured by other human beings. "Man is a wolf not a man to another man," Plautus says, "when he doesn't know what he is like."[18] So Plautus ascribes evil in human affairs to unknowing. Evil is the mystery of lovelessness, a word that means "unloving, unloved, unlovely," but the mystery of it is an unknowing. When knowing comes, there is an experience of horror. "Did he live his life again in every detail of desire, temptation, and surrender during that moment of complete knowledge?" Joseph Conrad asks in *Heart of Darkness*. "He cried in a whisper at some image, at some vision— he cried out twice, a cry that was no more than a breath—The horror! The horror!"[19]

Passing over then, if Plautus is on the right track, is the answer to evil, passing over into other lives, other cultures, other religions, coming to know what the other is like, and coming back with new insight to my own life, my own culture, my own religion. Sometimes, it is true, passing over is a disillusionment. When I am drawn to the mysterious life I perceive in another, "an unknown life" (*une vie inconnue*)[20] as Proust calls it, I pass over into that life only to find it is quite an ordinary life. It is like Ordinary Time in the liturgical year as distinct from the Advent or the Christmas or the Lenten or the Easter season. There is after all a mysterious life there in the ordinary but it is hidden. "The true paradises," as Proust says, "are paradises we have lost."[21]

So I perceive a mysterious life in another, "an unknown life," but when I pass over I find it is an ordinary life and it becomes for me a paradise lost. All the same, there is a depth of life in ordinary life, a mystery that "shows itself and at the same time withdraws." It shows itself when it draws me to the other, and it withdraws when I pass over into the life of the other, and yet it is still there hidden. Heidegger is speaking of technology, saying "The meaning pervading technology hides itself," when he defines mystery as "that which shows itself and at the same time withdraws,"[22] but what he says seems true of human relations, the meaning pervading human relations hides itself. What is the meaning? It may be like that of nature as Einstein saw it, "Nature hides her secret because of her essential loftiness" (or "the loftiness of her essence").

It is the human relation to nature that is the meaning pervading technology. Letting be and openness to the mystery, the relation Heidegger proposes, is also a relation to death, letting the things be that are being taken away in death and openness to the mystery that shows itself and at the same time withdraws in death, the mystery of eternal life. Death is the prime example of "the clumsy, wasteful, blundering, low, and horridly cruel works of nature." Eternal life, on the other hand, is God at work in life and death, the eternal at work in time. I take it, therefore, that eternal life is essentially a relation, a relationship with God the eternal. As I understand it, eternal life belongs to those entering into the relation of Jesus with God, "Now he is not God of the dead, but of the living: for all live to him."[23]

"Alone with the Alone,"[24] that is how Plotinus' vision of emanation culminates. If I combine emanation and evolution in a vision of all coming from God and returning to God, thinking of the relation of Jesus with his God, I come to something like that sentence in Luke, "for all live to him" (RSV, or in KJ "for all live unto him"). It is a vision in which all are alive. It is like that moment in Tolkien's trilogy where Sam wakes up to find he is alive. "I thought you were dead!" he says to Gandalf. "But then I thought I was dead myself. Is everything sad going to come untrue?"[25] It is a vision of joy. To be alone with the Alone is to be unalone, and if all are alive to the Alone, it is to be very unalone. But the point of "alone with the Alone" is to be one with the One, and that is the meaning of "the cloud of unknowing in the which a soul is oned with God." I take it then that to go "into the darkness with love," into the darkness of unknowing, even into the darkness of dying, is to "live unto him."

I think of the words King George VI quoted from M. Louise Haskins,

> I said to the man who stood at the gate of the year, Give me a light that I may tread safely into the unknown. And he replied, Go out into the darkness and put your hand into the hand

of God. That shall be to you better than light and safer than a known way.[26]

Christ is the man who stands at the gate of the year, and I want him to give me a light that I may tread safely into the unknown of living and dying, especially into the unknown of my dying. And he tells me to go out into the darkness of my unknowing, even into the darkness of my dying, and put my hand into the hand of God, into the hand of God-with-us, my companion in life, and that shall be to me better than light, better than some kind of certainty I could rely on instead of God, and safer than a known way, safer than a familiar path I have already taken.

What I am doing if I put my hand into the hand of God is trusting God beyond my own understanding. If knowing is taking things in and loving is going out to things, then I cannot take God in by knowing but I can go out to God by loving. Trusting God beyond my own understanding is going out to God by loving. "Beyond logic, beyond reason, beyond hope. Trust me,"[27] the High One says in Patricia McKillip's trilogy. I feel in facing the prospect of death I am trusting God "beyond logic, beyond reason, beyond hope." Certainly I am trusting God beyond my own understanding. As I understand it, "God is spirit"[28] as Jesus says to the woman at the well, and God acts spiritually, illumining the mind and kindling the heart, and so eternal life is the life of the spirit, the life of knowing and loving. Can our inner life, the life of the spirit, survive the death of our outer life? That is the question of eternal life. To believe it can is to trust God beyond my own understanding, beyond my experience of inner and outer life.

Still, there is a knowing that comes of loving, a knowing that comes of going "into the darkness with love." This knowing is what Wittgenstein calls "the mystical": "Not *how* the world is, is the mystical, but *that* it is," C. K. Ogden translates; "The feeling of the world as a limited whole is the mystical feeling"; and "There is indeed the inexpressible. This *shows* itself; it is the mystical."[29] Eternal life connects with the wonder of existence, *that* I am, as if I were chosen to exist, with the feeling of the world as a limited whole ("In sorrow we must go, but not in despair," Tolkien has Aragorn say on his deathbed. "Behold! we are not bound for ever to the circles of the world, and beyond them is more than memory. Farewell!")[30] and with the distinction between saying and showing, eternal life "shows itself."

As mystery, eternal life "shows itself and at the same time withdraws." It shows itself, I would say, in Christ in his relation with God, shows itself when we enter into the relation ourselves, making his God our God, "my Father and your Father," as he says to Mary Magdalene, "my God and your God."[31] At the same time it withdraws because assurance comes not from relying on the experience itself but only from relying on God. The experience is that of the life of the spirit, the life of knowing and loving, but the assurance that this inner life can survive the death of our outer life comes only from relying on God, relying on the God of Jesus. In fact, those words of his are an expression of that assurance, "I am ascending to my Father and your Father, to my God and your God." All the same, eternal life is something we experience already on this side of death, being on a journey with God in time and so relating to God-with-us.

"God requires the heart"[32] as is said in the Talmud. God answers my prayers but requires my heart. My vision quest combines the ancient vision of emanation of all from the One with the modern vision of evolution of all towards the One in the single image of a journey with God in time, "My presence will go with you, and I will give you rest."[33] That is my hope, that God will go with me, and that God will give me rest. My fear and sadness are of death; my desire and gladness are of eternal life.

The Riddle of Eternal Life

Is a riddle solved by the fact that I survive for ever? Is this eternal life not as egnimatic as out present one? The solution of the riddle of life in space and time lies outside space and time.

—Ludwig Wittgenstein

◆ There are three questions, taken together, that outline the riddle of eternal life:

Am I my world?
Am I my time?
Am I my body?

No to each, I am *in* my world, I am *in* my time, I am *in* my body, outlines the possibility of eternal life. Actually Wittgenstein says "I am my world," and "Am I my time?" is the question Heidegger comes to at the end of his lecture on time, and he wants to answer "Yes,"[1] but I want to answer "No" and thus to open the way to eternal life.

"I have had my world as in my tyme,"[2] the Wife of Bath says in Chaucer's *Canterbury Tales*. I take it she means she has had a very full life. At any rate she uses those phrases "my world" and "my time" that I am using in my questions. As for the third phrase, "my body," I think of something a woman friend of mine once said, "A woman is very conscious of being in a body." I suppose she meant that a woman is inevitably conscious of things like the menstrual cycle, whereas a man can be relatively oblivious of the body's cycles. My world, my time, my body then are possible answers to the question "Who am I?" It may be, though, "Within our whole universe the story only has authority to answer that cry of heart of its characters," as Isak Dinesen says, "that one cry of heart of each of them: *Who am I?*"[3]

To say my story answers the cry of heart *Who am I?* is very close to saying I am my time. "We can know more than we can tell,"[4] as Michael Polanyi says, and we can tell the story, but we can know more, as he says, by dwelling in the particulars of what we know. This seems to agree with what I am saying, I am not my world but am in my world, I am not my time but am in my time, I am not my body but am in my body. By dwelling in the particulars of my world, my time, my body, I can know more than I can tell in telling my story. What then of eternal life? It is not among the particulars of my world, of my time, of my body. Its possibility is in my indwelling.

"Eternal life belongs to those who live in the present,"[5] Wittgenstein says. I want to say *Eternal life belongs to those who live in the presence.* I find the presence in my world (as in Henry Vaughan's poem "The World") like a great circle of life and light and love; I find the presence in my time (as in Plato's dialogue *Timaeus*) as "a changing image of eternity"; and I find the presence even in my body if I may see the human body as a temple.

Am I My World?

I saw Eternity the other night,
Like a great ring of pure and endless light,
All calm, as it was bright.

Thus Henry Vaughan begins his poem "The World."[6] That great ring of pure and endless light I take to be the same as the great circle of love the old man of the desert described to Lawrence of Arabia, "The love is from God and of God and towards God." I see that circle running through life and light and love in my world. I am speaking of course of a vision on this vision quest of mine, a way of seeing life and light and love. The three metaphors are from the Gospel of John, life and light and love. To see them as from and of and towards God suggests the vision of emanation, the *from,* and that of evolution, the *towards.* The *of,* that the life and light and love are of God, suggests the eternal presence. If the great circle is like the circulation of the blood and God is like the heart, everything coming from God and returning to God, there is an apogee, a point farthest from God. "Even love must pass through loneliness,"[7] Wendell Berry says, describing such a circle, and light must pass through darkness, we could say, and life must pass through death.

Eternal life, therefore, means living in this great circle of life and light and love, passing through death, passing through darkness, passing through loneliness.

> They are all gone into the world of light,
> And I alone sit lingering here,

Henry Vaughan begins another poem.[8] They have all passed through death to life, through darkness to light, he is saying, and I am still here, passing through loneliness. I can relate to his feeling here, remembering a dream I once had of a friend who had recently died, a woman friend who died of breast cancer, how in my dream she appeared joyous and radiant, in a white garment with bare feet, how she called my name and then turned, looking back over her shoulder, as if I were to follow. I took the dream not as a call to death so much as an invitation to follow like Dante with her as my Beatrice. "They are all gone into the world of light" seems to mean they have all returned to God, "And I alone sit lingering here" to mean I have not yet returned, though I am on the great circle that comes from God and returns to God.

There is a "poetry of the universe," we may say if we may speak of a great circle of life and light and love and of a journey like Dante's through loneliness to love, through darkness to light, through death to life. I hesitate to give the poetry a mathematical interpretation (though I have done so elsewhere, speaking of the Dante-Riemann universe).[9] I feel better just letting the poetry be poetry or what Vico calls "poetic wisdom." My calling, I believe, is to wisdom not to science, and to poetic wisdom at that. If we think of poetry as taking its origin in "emotion recollected in tranquillity,"[10] then the emotions I am recollecting here are the fear and sadness of death and the desire and gladness of eternal life. Poetic wisdom is insight into these emotions, putting them together on this great circle of life and light and love. Dante's journey, as he says at the end, is "high fantasy" (*alta fantasia*),[11] an exercise of imagination, but there is a profound truth in it. Poetic wisdom is "insight into image," insight into the high fantasy of this journey to the event horizon, to the limits of our experience, uncovering the truth of the great circle, how the love really is from God and of God and towards God, what we can know more than we can tell, the truth of the relationship underlying the story of the journey.

"Flee fro the prees, and dwelle with sothfastnesse,"[12] Chaucer says. Flee from the crowd, that is, and dwell with truth. That is how to live in the eternal presence, to live in the great circle of life and light and love. I can see a three-stage process of coming to this, for instance in the life of Saint Augustine, as he goes from living before others (his days as a rhetorician) to living before self (his *Soliloquies*) to living before God (his *Confessions*), and at each stage there is a vision of the world.

When I am living before others, I am living in hope and fear, the hope of acceptance and the fear of rejection. My care is of what I am to others. My world is the world of others. Is there a vision of the world in this? And am I my world, if this is my world? Surely I am *in* my world too if my world is of others. There is a vision of the world in this too,

All the world's a stage,
And all the men and women merely players.[13]

It is a vision indeed if you take into account the question Ben Jonson asked, if all the men and women are merely players who are the spectators? And Shakespeare's answer, the men and women themselves are both the spectators and the players. There is even a scientific vision in this, us as observers as well as observed phenomena in the world.

If we were only players, we would live before others, but if we are also spectators, they live before us and we judge them (or suspend judgement on them). So in a given human relationship I live before the other person but the other also lives before me. If I suspend judgement, I am able to *pass over* to the other and assume the other's standpoint. Then I am able to *come back* to my own standpoint with new insight. If I do not suspend judgement, on the other hand, if I judge, I remain in my standpoint as a spectator and the other remains in their standpoint as a player. "Judge not, that you be not judged,"[14] the words in the Sermon on the Mount, seem to call then for a suspension of judgement and for passing over and for coming back with new insight. If I judge, I remain fixed in my standpoint as a spectator, and to that extent I am judged, remaining fixed also in my standpoint as a player.

A vision of the world playacting was the motto of the Globe Theatre, as if the whole globe were a theatre, *totus mundus agit histrionem,* and these were Ben Jonson's comments,

If, but stage actors, all the world displays,
Where shall we find spectators of their plays?

and Shakespeare's reply,

Little, or much, of what we see we do;
We're all both actors and spectators too.[15]

There is a strong suggestion of imitation in that first line of Shakespeare's, "Little, or much, of what we see we do," as in "Monkey see, monkey do." Living before others, we live in imitation of others, but not in some profound imitation of a transcendent archetype, like *the imitation of Christ*. We live rather in straightforward imitation of what we see.

Imitation of a transcendent archetype, as in Plato's vision of emanation, becomes as it were a conscious project in living before self and living before God. Imitation of Christ, for instance, means going from living before others and imitating them to following Christ and taking to heart his "words of eternal life," letting such words speak to the heart ("Lord, to whom shall we go? You have the words of eternal life").[16] It means going from living by "mimetic desire," as René Girard calls it, where we see what others want and want what they want, to living by heart's desire where "heart speaks to heart" and we follow the heart.

> May I know me!
> May I know thee!

Noverim me! Noverim te![17] the prayer of Saint Augustine's *Soliloquies* is perhaps the prayer of all soliloquy and of living before self. As a prayer it seems to belong already to the standpoint of living before God. Yet it is a brief exclamation and not like the sustained prayer of Augustine's *Confessions,* written ten years later. It is an expression of the heart's desire to know self and to know God. What is the heart's desire? I take it to be a desire to know and be known, to love and be loved. It is the yearning in the deep loneliness of the human condition, the yearning to be known and loved, the yearning to be unalone and so also to know and to love. The heart's desire is eternal life. "And this is eternal life," it is said in the Gospel of John, "that they know thee the only true God and Jesus Christ whom thou hast sent."[18]

Is there a difference here? To know me and to know thee/to know thee and to know Christ. There is an overlap, to know thee, and there is a difference, between knowing me and knowing Christ. It is perhaps the difference between living before self and living before God. There is a vision of the world in knowing me and knowing thee. Knowing is remembering, Augustine says in his *Soliloquies,* but he takes this back in his *Retractations* and speaks instead of "the presence of the light of eternal reason."[19] The Platonic doctrine of recollection, that knowing is remembering, seems to go with living before self, and Augustine's own doctrine of divine illumination to go with living before God. At any rate, there is a vision of the world in recollection where my world is the world of my remembrance.

> What seest thou else
> In the dark backward and abysm of time?[20]

Prospero asks Miranda. To know myself is to remember my life; to know God is to remember God.

Living before myself, I know myself insofar as I remember my life. I can't leap over my own shadow, get on top of myself and understand myself from the outside, for I am myself, and there is no Archimedean point outside my world where I can stand. I am a mystery then to myself, though I can recall my past life, and that is what points me on to living before God. Augustine in his *Soliloquies* goes through a process of reasoning not unlike that of Descartes, "I think therefore I am." He is in dialogue with his own reason. After his praying "May I know me! May I know thee!" his reason asks him "You who wish to know yourself, do you know you exist?" "I do" he answers . . ."You know that you think?" "I do" he answers again.[21] I suppose this is knowing himself, and I could say I know myself in this way, knowing I think and knowing I am. Augustine's interest, though, and mine too, is in eternal life. "Do you know that you are immortal?" his reason asks. "No" he replies.

Here is where knowing God and remembering God comes in if "all live unto him." Wittgenstein formulates the idea of eternal life as a riddle rather than an answer to a riddle:

The temporal immortality of the human soul, that is
to say, its eternal survival after death, is not only
in no way guaranteed, but this assumption in the first
place will not do for us what we always tried to make
it do. Is a riddle solved by the fact that I survive forever?
Is this eternal life not as enigmatic as the present one?
The solution of the riddle of space and time lies *outside*
space and time.[22]

It lies in the transcendence of God, I think he means, and the transcendence of God corresponds to the transcendence of our longing, how our longing always goes *beyond* every finite object. So it
is always a mistake to let our longing get fixed on someone or
something finite, for it will always go beyond that finite object and
the relationship with it will fail. Still, it is possible to have a relationship with another or with others by sharing in the longing and
going on the journey together. Living before myself, I live then in
the transcendence of my own longing.

That transcendence of longing is what Augustine is talking
about, it seems, at the beginning of his *Confessions,* "our heart is
restless until it rests in you,"[23] and that is what leads into the standpoint of living before God. What happens in this standpoint, to
judge from his *Confessions,* is that the transcendence of longing
finds expression in prayer. In Goethe's autobiography, *Poetry and
Truth,* the method is to turn the truth of the life into poetry. Here in
Augustine's the truth of the life is the restless heart and the poetry
of the life is prayer and repose in God. There is a conversation with
ourselves going on all the time, we could say, a conversation about
our concerns, our hopes and our fears, and when we let it become a
conversation with God, bringing to God our hopes and our fears,
bringing all our concerns to God as in the Psalms, we move into the
standpoint of living before God and we find repose in God, an
inner peace not unlike "emotion recollected in tranquillity."

Truth and poetry, if I turn the truth of my own life, my fear
and sadness, my desire and gladness, into the poetry of prayer,
I find myself in the standpoint of living before God. As I said, my

fear and sadness is of death; my desire and gladness is of eternal life. Every day I say this prayer, based on the psalm "The Lord is my shepherd,"

> O Lord, go with me
> and be my guide,
> in my most need
> be by my side:
> if you are guiding me
> I shall not want,
> if you are guarding me
> I shall not fear,
> though I am walking
> in the valley of the shadow
> of my dying,
> you are walking with me,
> and when I am not
> you will have taken me.[24]

In the first lines I am echoing "Everyman, I will go with thee and be thy guide, in thy most need to go by thy side," and in the last lines I am echoing Genesis, "Enoch walked with God; and he was not, for God took him."[25]

Turning truth into poetry leads for me into a further step of turning words into music. I see a parallel between Stravinsky's *Symphony of Psalms,* where he sets words from three psalms to music (Psalms 38, 39, and 150), and Augustine's *Confessions,* where the words especially of three psalms are echoed (Psalms 4, 41, and 138).[26] Setting words to music, for instance the words of the prayer above, I find myself using traditional melodies of Gregorian chant, in this instance the melody of Kyrie XII, and harmonizing them in four parts, using Nicolas Slonimsky's method of harmonization in major triads. The resulting song can be sung in four parts or as a solo using the melodic line in the treble. Bach's chorales are mostly harmonizations like this of traditional melodies, only his chorales have more counterpoint.

The Good Shepherd

A final step, after turning the truth of a life into the poetry and
setting the words to music, is to turn the song into dance. I have always left this to others, letting dancers dance to my songs, though
I see something essential in it, loving God "with all your might" as
in the words "David danced before the Lord with all his might."[27]
The command is to love "with all your heart, and with all your soul,
and with all your might." To turn the truth of a life into the poetry
of prayer is to love "with all your heart"; to set the words to music
is to love "with all your soul"; and to turn the song into dance is to
love "with all your might." There is a wholeness of human existence here. And if we add, as in the Gospels, to love "with all your
mind," that has to do with the truth of the life itself. There is a
vision of human wholeness here and implicitly of the world, the
macrocosm in terms of the human microcosm. And it is the question of eternal life, "What shall I do to inherit eternal life?"[28]

Yet is it enough to turn truth into poetry, to set words to music,
to turn song into dance? "For poetry makes nothing happen," as
W. H. Auden says in his poem "In Memory of W. B. Yeats."[29] I suppose eternal life doesn't depend on making something happen. It is
true, "What shall I do to inherit eternal life?" implies that I must do
something, but the answer is to love, not to make something happen. To love with all my heart and with all my soul and with all my
might is to be whole in my relationship with God and with others.
I think of those words of Goethe that are the epigraph of Martin
Buber's *I and Thou,*

So, waiting, I have won from you the end:
God's presence in each element.[30]

Being whole in my relation with another person, he is saying, I
come into the presence of God, and into Goethe's vision of the
world, "God's presence in each element."

If eternal life belongs to those who live in the presence, then it
belongs to those who live in the *I and thou* relationship with God
and with others. "Do this, and you will live."[31] If you are whole in

your relation with God and with others, you will find "God's presence in each element." Eternal life, according to the Gospel of
John, belongs to those who live in the relation of Jesus with God,
"my Father and your Father," as he says to Mary Magdalene, "my
God and your God." I take it then that eternal life is essentially a
relationship, that it means living in a relationship, heart and soul.
What is more, I can know this relationship. "We can know more
than we can tell." It is more than I can tell in telling my story, and
that seems to have a bearing on survival after death, on survival
after the ending of my story.

Dwelling in the particulars of our relationship is how we can
know more than we can tell. The particulars in the prayer above
are especially "guiding" and "guarding." Of course I am telling of
them in the prayer, but I can know more of them than I can tell,
dwelling in them. Guiding, first of all, what I can tell of guiding is
the story, I can tell my story and see myself being led step by step,
one step at a time. What is more, I can tell of my hope of being
guided, "go with me and be my guide, in my most need be by my
side" and "if you are guiding me I shall not want." What I can
know, more than I can tell, is the relationship itself. My knowing
this relationship is my sense of being led. Guarding then, what I
can tell of guarding too is my story, and I can see myself being
guarded in the things and situations of my life. And I can tell of
my hope of being guarded, "if you are guarding me I shall not fear,
though I am walking in the valley of the shadow of my dying, you
are walking with me, and when I am not you will have taken me."
What I can know, again, is the relationship, and my knowing this is
my sense of being guarded.

So instead of saying "I am my world" I want to say "I am *in* my
world, and I am guided and guarded," so as in the psalm, "I shall
not want . . . I will fear no evil . . . and I will dwell in the house of
the Lord for ever."[32] If I were describing my world mathematically,
as I have done elsewhere, I would speak of "the event horizon,"[33]
the limit of my field of vision. "Our life is endless in the way that
our visual field is without limit," Wittgenstein says, meaning we

cannot perceive the limit of our field of vision and we cannot perceive the limit of our life in death, for "Death is not an event of life. Death is not lived through."[34] But I want to say death *is* an event of life, death *is* lived through, and there *is* a limit of our field of vision, "the event horizon," and thus a world that is beyond our vision.

Am I My Time?

Time itself is a horizon, Heidegger says in the preface to his *Being and Time*, "the possible horizon for any understanding whatsoever of Being."[35] To say there is "an event horizon" is to say there is a horizon to what we can observe "in the dark backward and abysm of time," for when we look into the night sky we are looking into the past, given that light travels at a speed that is finite. To say time itself is a horizon is to say there is a horizon not only to observation but even to understanding. But when we feel the wonder of existence, gazing into the night sky, "the mystical," when we perceive Being, "not *how* the world is but *that* it is," we feel an eternal presence in time, it seems to me, and then it is that time seems "a changing image of eternity."

"If the philosopher asks about time," however, "then he has resolved *to understand time in terms of time,*" and not in terms of eternity, Heidegger says in his lecture on time, for "The philosopher does not believe."[36] All the same, he quotes from the *Confessions* of Saint Augustine, who does believe and who "pursued the question so far as to ask whether spirit itself is time,"[37] and Heidegger himself pursues the question so far as to ask "Am I my time?" To say "Yes, I am my time" is then to see time as "the possible horizon for any understanding whatsoever of Being." To say "No, I am *in* my time," as I want to do, is to open the way to eternal life and to thinking of time in terms of eternity. Augustine does try to understand time in terms of time in conversation with himself, but he tries to understand time in terms of eternity in conversation with

God. There is a shift here from the standpoint before self to the standpoint before God.

There is a shift also in Heidegger's later thinking from time as a horizon to time as "the lighting-up of the self-concealing" (*die Lichtung des Sichverbergens*)[38] That connects with his idea of mystery as "that which shows itself and at the same time withdraws." All this comes close to the idea that time is "a changing image of eternity": time is the lighting-up of self-concealing eternity, and eternity is a mystery that shows itself and at the same time withdraws in time. But Heidegger does not mention eternity here. He is thinking rather of the presence of Being: time is the lighting-up of self-concealing Being, and Being is a mystery that shows itself and at the same time withdraws in time. He is thinking, as always, in terms of Being and time. Yet what is Being? "Not *how* the world is but *that* it is." To come to a sense of eternal life and an eternal presence in time we have to make the shift that Saint Augustine made, from the standpoint of living before self to that of living before God.

I originally thought the *Confessions* of Saint Augustine were written entirely from the standpoint of prayer and living before God, but I find in his discussion of time in book 11 he shifts back for a while into the standpoint before himself and then shifts again into the standpoint before God. Actually he shifts back and forth between meditation and prayer. When he is before himself he is meditating on time in terms of time, but when he is before God he is praying on time in terms of eternity. Prayer too, as Saint Thomas Aquinas says, is an act of the intellect.[39]

"What is time?" Saint Augustine asks. "Provided that no one asks me, I know. If I want to explain it to an inquirer, I do not know."[40] If I ask myself what time is, I run into the same paradox of knowing and not knowing. This is another instance of what Polanyi says, "we can know more than we can tell." We can tell time, for instance I can tell now that it is ten minutes after four in the afternoon, but we can know more than we can tell of time, for we can know our relationship with time, that we are *in* time. Or at any rate that question that Heidegger poses, "are we ourselves time?" comes up here and has to do with our relationship with time. Are we ourselves time, as he says, or are we *in* time, as I want to say? If we know this relationship, and I think we do, and know we are *in* time, it is more than we can tell when we tell time, and knowing more than we can tell leaves us in the situation Augustine describes, "Provided that no one asks me, I know. If I want to explain to an inquirer, I do not know."

Is time a measurement? That is the question Augustine gets into as he goes on to talk about measuring time. I think of Einstein's theory of relativity and the notion of time as a dimension. There are the three dimensions of space and time therefore is a fourth dimension. This is indeed a theory of time as a measurement. It is, we could say, a space theory of time, where time is assimilated to space, and it has been criticized for that, for instance by Henri Bergson in his philosophy of creative evolution where the essential characteristic he finds in time is novelty, that something new is always happening. All the same, the theory of relativity and of time as a fourth dimension has become well established and generally accepted in physics. Heidegger too in his lecture on time casts a cold eye on the idea of time as a dimension, because he wants to say we ourselves are time, and that is what he sees Augustine coming to who "pursued the question so far as to ask whether spirit itself is time."

Is time "a distension in the soul"?[41] That is the question Augustine actually comes to in the passage Heidegger is quoting. Why "a distension in the soul"? As I understand him, Augustine is saying time is past and present and future, but the past no longer exists and the future does not yet exist. So where is the past and the future? The past is there in "the remembrance of things past" as Shakespeare calls it in his Sonnets, and the future is there in "dreaming on things to come."[42] So past and future are in the soul remembering and dreaming. And if time is an extension that can be measured, it must be "a distension in the soul." Or rather this is the question Augustine comes to, Is time "a distension in the soul"? Does this mean we ourselves are time or I am my time? No, I think it means that I am dwelling in my time, remembering things past and dreaming on things to come.

To understand time we have to go on "from here to Eternity," to shift with Saint Augustine from the standpoint before self to that before God, where time is seen in relation to eternity. Considering only what Augustine says from the standpoint before self, Bertrand Russell says "Saint Augustine, whose absorption in the sense of sin led him to excessive subjectivity, was content to substitute subjective time for the time of history and physics," but Kurt Gödel, on the other hand, has argued from his own investigations into the theory of relativity that there is no "objective lapse of time" and thus time is essentially subjective time, and Wittgenstein, after quoting Augustine on knowing and not knowing time, says "Something we know when no one asks us, but no longer know when we are supposed to give an account of it, is something we need to *remind* ourselves of"[43] I think if we move with Saint Augustine from before self to before God, we do the reminding and find that time is "a changing image of eternity."

How does Saint Augustine get "from here to Eternity"? I find the answer in Marcel Proust's conclusion to his long *Remembrance of Things Past*:

> If, at least, there were granted me time enough to complete my work, I would not fail to stamp it with the seal of that Time the understanding of which was this day so forcibly impressing itself upon me, and I would therein describe men—even should that give them the semblance of monstrous creatures—as occupying in Time a place far more considerable than the so restricted one allotted to them in space, a place, on the contrary, extending boundlessly since, giant-like, reaching far back into the years,

they touch simultaneously epochs of their lives—with countless intervening days between—so widely separated from one another in Time.[44]

This is what Augustine means by "a distension in the soul" or actually "a distension of the mind" or "of the spirit" (*distentio animi*). We come before God by recollection. Or the fully recollected person is before God. Yet Proust himself is a secular instance. So I should say we come before God by recollection if we believe, and our eternity is all time recollected.

There is "a sense of eternity,"[45] as Proust says, in recollection, and it is the recollection of his life that carries Augustine "from here to Eternity." It is true, Augustine does not quote those words from Plato, as far as I know, calling time "a changing image of eternity," but the idea seems pervasive in his thinking, and his understanding of time seems to be an insight into the image that time is, seeing unchanging eternity in the changing image of time. If I recollect my own life, writing a memoir like Augustine, I find I come to an image of my life as a whole and an insight into the image. I see my life as a process of learning to love, according to the command, "with all your heart, and with all your soul, and with all your might," and as is added in the Gospels "with all your mind." That for me is an insight into the changing image of my time.

Insight into the changing image of time uncovers what Kierkegaard calls "an eternal self" and "an eternal consciousness." This eternal self, it seems to me, is the whole human person who comes to light in loving "with all your heart, and with all your soul, and with all your might" and "with all your mind." An eternal self? An eternal consciousness? "If there were no eternal consciousness in a man," Kierkegaard says in *Fear and Trembling*, "if at the foundation of all lay only a wildly seething power which writhing with obscure passions produced everything that is great and everything that is insignificant, if a bottomless void never satiated lay hidden beneath all—what then would life be but despair?"[46] It is this eternal self, this eternal consciousness, that is being imaged in my time, if my time is a changing image of eternity. This eternal self, this eternal consciousness, is the eternal in us. If most people live lives of "quiet desperation," as Thoreau says, the quiet desperation is due, according to Kierkegaard, to being unaware of having an eternal self, for "what then would life be but despair?"

It is true, I could say "I am my time," as Heidegger wants to say, and yet also say "time is a changing image of eternity," but then eternity for me would be simply a timeless paradigm of my life. If eternity is alive, on the other hand, if God is God of the living, as Christ argues with the Sadducees, and all are alive to God, then eternity for me is an eternal self, an eternal consciousness, and I have to say "I am *in* my time." So to say my time is "a changing image of eternity" is to say my life is like a cinema, a motion picture, a changing image, but the person who is being shown in this changing image is an eternal self. As Kierkegaard understands it, the self is a relation that relates to itself. By relating to myself and willing to be myself, he says, I am grounded transparently in God. It is that transparent grounding in God that is the source of eternal life. It is God who is eternal, and we are eternal in our relationship with God.

"A single minute released from the chronological order of time has recreated in us the human being similarly released, in order that he may sense the minute," Proust writes in *Remembrance of Things Past*. "And one comprehends readily how such a one can be confident in his joy; even though the mere taste of a madeleine does not seem to contain logical justification for this joy, it is easy to understand that the word 'death' should have no meaning for him; situated outside the scope of time, what could he fear from the future?"[47] So recollection is an answer to death for Proust, and bringing time to mind overcomes the lapsing of time. For me, though, the only real answer is eternal life. For Proust the taste of a madeleine sets off the whole *Remembrance of Things Past*. For me, though, "the remembrance of things past" and "dreaming on things to come" still leaves me naked in the face of death. I remember writing my first book and coming to the conclusion, after considering the many answers to death in the history of thought, and feeling those words of the Gospel speak to my heart, "he who believes in me, though he die, yet shall he live, and whoever lives and believes in me shall never die."[48]

Eternal life, according to these words, belongs to those who believe in Jesus Christ, and believing in him, as I understand it, means making his God my God, "my Father and your Father," as he says to Mary Magdalene, "my God and your God," and his God is God of the living, as he argues with the Sadducees, God to whom all are alive. So it is by believing in the God of the living, by entering into the unconditional relationship that Jesus has with Abba his God that I hope to have eternal life. It is an *I and thou* with God, as Martin Buber says in *I and Thou*, speaking of Jesus, "For it is the *I* of unconditional relation in which the man calls his *Thou* Father in such a way that he himself is simply Son, and nothing else but Son," and yet "every man can say *Thou* and is then *I*, every man can say Father and is then Son."[49] Eternal life then is a relationship, an *I and thou* relationship with God.

So it is true, after all, recollection is an answer to death, if we carry recollection far enough, not stopping like Proust at the standpoint of the person before self but going on like Saint Augustine to the standpoint of the person before God. "Thinking is thanking" (*Denken ist danken*), the mystic saying of the seventeenth century that Heidegger always quotes, is from this standpoint before God, though there is a shortfall in Heidegger's way of taking it. "Noble-mindedness would be the nature of thinking and thereby of thanking," the Scholar says in "Conversation on a Country Path," and Heidegger answers "of that thinking which does not have to thank for something, but only thanks for being allowed to thank."[50] I want to say rather that recollection of a life can be a thinking that is thanking, like "counting your blessings," like Saint Augustine's *Confessions*, which are confessions not just of sin but of praise.

"If by eternity is understood not endless temporal duration but timelessness," Wittgenstein says, "then he lives eternally who lives in the present," or in another translation "eternal life belongs to those who live in the present."[51] Living in the present is the opposite of recollection. That is why I want to say, rather, that eternal life belongs to those who live in the presence, for recollection means living in the presence. So when Dag Hammarskjöld says in his diary at the turning point in his life, "For all that has been— Thanks! To all that shall be Yes!"[52] he is living in the presence, relating to the past with his "Thanks!" and to the future with his "Yes!" Indeed the "Thanks!" and "Yes!" are to Someone, and he is relating to past and future in the presence of God. It is not enough to say the past exists no longer and the future does not yet exist, it seems to me, and only the present exists (the assumptions of "an objective lapse of time"), but it is necessary to relate in a positive way to the past and the future, to all that has been and all that shall be. It is necessary if we are to be whole human beings.

"Eternity is the simultaneous and complete possession of infinite life,"[53] Boethius says in *The Consolation of Philosophy,* finding consolation in his unhappiness by seeing life under the joyful aspect of eternity where everything is lasting instead of the sorrowful aspect of time where everything is passing. "For of all suffering from Fortune," he says, "the unhappiest misfortune is to have known a happy fortune." [54] In every ill-turn of fortune, he is saying, the most unhappy sort of misfortune is to have been happy. Sadness goes with loss and loss goes with time, with the lapse of time. If there is only time, then loss is final and sadness inescapable, but if there is eternity, then there is a gladness that goes deeper than sadness. Where to find that eternity, that gladness? I want to find it in the standpoint of the person before God, but there are other ways: in the timeless moment, in time recollected, and in a vision like that of Nietzsche of an eternal recurrence of things and situations in a finite universe,

The world is deep,
And deeper than the day could read.
Deep is its woe—,

Joy—deeper still than grief can be:
Woe saith: Hence! Go!
But joys all want eternity—,
—Want deep, profound eternity![55]

All these visions of eternity promise joy: joy in the timeless moment, joy in time recollected, joy in the eternal recurrence of things and situations. For me, though, joy is in the standpoint of the person before God. The love of God, as Spinoza says, is simply joy at the thought of God, for me joy at the thought of being on a journey with God in time, joy at the thought of the great circle that is from and of and towards God—the "with God" is there in the "of God." If joy is "deeper still than grief can be," it is indeed because "joys all want eternity, want deep, profound eternity," but eternity for me is God's, "like a great ring of pure and endless light," as Henry Vaughan says, "all calm, as it was bright."

As I contemplate these visions of eternity, the timeless moment, time recollected, the eternal recurrence, and the great circle of life and light and love, I think of *Einstein's Dreams*, a novel about visions of time, and I realize each vision of time is also a vision of eternity, and each vision of eternity is also a vision of time. "I want to understand time because I want to get close to The Old One," Einstein says to his friend Besso in the story. Besso nods but he says there are problems: "For one, perhaps The Old One is not interested in getting close to his creations, intelligent or not. For another, it is not obvious that knowledge is closeness. For yet another, this time project could be too big for a twenty-six year old."[56] This is what I want too, "to get close to The Old One," to get close to God. I am hoping The Old One is interested in getting close to his creations, and hoping knowledge will turn out to be closeness, and hoping too this vision quest is not too big for me.

I realize my vision of the great circle of life and light and love is a vision of time as well as eternity. If eternity is the great circle, time is the moving point describing the circle. Is this great circle the same as the eternal recurrence? No, it is not simply a repeating cycle but is from and of and towards God. "In my beginning is my end," as T. S. Eliot says at the beginning of one of his *Four Quartets,* and "In my end is my beginning" as he says at the end.[57] My beginning is in God, and my end is in God, and God is with me on the way from the beginning to the end.

Am I My Body?

Had we but world enough, and time,
This coyness, Lady, were no crime,

Andrew Marvell says to his coy mistress, but we don't,

And yonder all before us lie
Deserts of vast eternity,

and our bodies are mortal, and we will die,

The grave's a fine and private place,
But none, I think, do there embrace.[58]

So the riddle of eternal life becomes that of our mortal bodies. Am I my body? If I am, then death is the end, but if I am *in* my body, then there is hope.

Am I my body? Is my brain my mind? That is another way of putting it, especially since neuroscientists have been equating the mind and the brain. There is a fallacy here, according to Peter Hacker, of taking the part for the whole, ascribing to the brain things that are properly ascribed to the person as a whole. Taking the part for the whole is a customary figure of speech, but it becomes a fallacy if it is taken no longer as a figure but as a fact. "Only of a human being," Wittgenstein says, "and what resembles (behaves like) a living human being can one say: it has sensations; it sees; is blind; hears; is deaf; is conscious or unconscious."[59]

My own approach is to ask still another question, Is matter a dimension? This was an idea that came to me when I was in my twenties, *matter is a dimension*. It is close, I realize now, to Descartes, who thought of matter as extension. At any rate, I wrote those many years ago to Erwin Schrödinger, the great physicist largely responsible for the wave theory in quantum mechanics, and I asked him if he thought the idea was workable. I got a one sentence reply, "Matter is *not* a dimension." So I put the idea aside. But in these later years it has come back to me and I have tried to work it out. "Everything that exists is situated," Max Jacob says in the preface to *The Dice Cup*, his prose poems. "Everything that's above matter is situated, matter itself is situated."[60] Everything is situated in space and time, he means, the four dimensions of the theory of relativity (he is talking about existence not about transcendence). *But does matter also situate?* That is my question. If it does, that means the brain situates the mind and the body situates the soul. At least on a purely physical level it seems true: on the small scale matter as particles is situated but as waves it situates, and on the large scale matter is situated in space and time but it also situates by curving or warping space and time.

Matter then is a dimension, I want to say, and I can even formulate it mathematically as DeBroglie waves on the small scale and as the curvature of space or of spacetime on the large scale. Yet can the simple idea of a dimension account for the great complexity of matter, from subatomic particles to neurons in the human brain? There has to be another factor besides matter, namely, form or structure. On the one hand, everything is made of everything else; on the other, everything has its own structure.

If matter situates, if the brain situates the mind, if the body situates the soul, then there is a connection between matter and memory. There is such a thing as "a memory theatre" or "a memory palace,"[61] an imaginative way of organizing memory, practised in the time of the Renaissance—Shakespeare may have had a memory theatre. It may be that the human brain, as studied by today's neuroscientists, is actually a memory theatre not unlike the imaginative ones of the Renaissance. The word "mind" means "memory" in common phrases like "time out of mind" or "keep in mind" or "bring to mind." I want to say the brain is not the mind but situates the mind. So we may consider the brain essentially a memory theatre. If I search for God in time and memory, like Saint Augustine in his *Confessions*, I am searching in that memory theatre.

If the body situates the soul, it makes sense to speak of bodily centers of the soul's functions, like the seven centers in Hindu tradition: at the base of the spinal column, at the base of the genital organ, in the lumbar region at the level of the navel, in the heart, in the throat, between the eyebrows, and at the top of the head, or like the four in Easter Christian mysticism (Hesychasm): between the eyebrows, in the mouth and throat, in the breast, and in the heart. In the Hindu tradition, as the life-force rises from one center to another there is a movement from existence to transcendence. In the Christian, there is a movement toward greater and greater inwardness in prayer. In both there is a hint of "immortality and freedom."[62] If I am my body, then my death is my end, but if my body situates my soul, then there is hope of eternal life,

> And when life's sweet fable ends,
> Soul and body part like friends;
> No quarrels, murmurs, no delay;
> A kiss, a sigh, and so away.[63]

Those hopeful and peaceful words of Richard Crashaw may make death sound too easy, "Soul and body part like friends"! Not so peaceful, always restless and seeking repose in God, Saint Augustine begins his book on memory (book 10 of his *Confessions*) with the prayer "May I know you, who know me,"[64] like the earlier prayer of his *Soliloquies*, "May I know me! May I know thee!" And he too goes through a movement from existence to transcendence. "Great is the power of memory, an awe-inspiring mystery, my God, a power of profound and infinite multiplicity. And this is mind, this is I myself," he says. "What then am I, my God? What is my nature?"[65] So he seems to be saying I am my mind, very far from saying I am my body, and yet I am a mystery to myself, for the mind is a mystery to itself, and memory is full of vast recesses. His existence is a mystery and he moves on to transcendence. "I will transcend even this my power which is called memory. I will rise beyond it to move towards you, sweet light." This is a few pages before the famous words, "Late have I loved you, beauty so old and so new: late have I loved you." He searches for God in time and memory, and he does indeed remember God, but he seems to find God at last beyond his memory. So God is in his memory, and yet beyond his memory. Indeed if the human brain is a memory theatre, as I have been suggesting, God is there and not there.

A memory theatre is a place of symbols or images, like *The Memory Palace of Matteo Ricci* described by Jonathan Spence.[66] If we think of the human brain as a memory theatre, it would not make sense to say with Michael Gazzaniga "The brain knows before you do."[67] For knowledge is not simply symbol or image but insight into image. What is more, it is the human being who knows. Materialism here, equating the mind and the brain, creates a confusion of imaging and knowing. If we go on to search for God in time and memory, like Saint Augustine, it becomes essential to discern between imaging and knowing, between stories of God and a relationship with God, realizing "we can know more than we can tell," we can know the relationship while telling the stories.

> This is the use of memory:
> For liberation—not less of love but expanding
> Of love beyond desire, and so liberation
> From the future as well as the past.[68]

T. S. Eliot writes in his *Four Quartets*, speaking of detachment in love. I think again of the prayer, "For all that has been—Thanks! To all that shall be—Yes!" There is a remembering of God in that "Thanks!" and "Yes!" as well as a liberation, becoming heart-free toward the past and the future and open to the mystery of eternal life. "Thinking is thanking" and for me thanking is in words and music. I divide my own memory theatre between words and music, linking words with the left brain and the right side of the body—I am right handed, and music with the right brain and the left side of the body—though I use both hands in playing the piano. I once had writer's cramp badly in my right arm after writing a book and tried to write with my left hand, but it looked like a child's scrawl. "The Kantian problem of the right and left hand which cannot be made to cover one another"[69] that Wittgenstein mentions seems to apply also to words and music. They cannot be made to cover one another, and yet they belong together, and maybe they point together to a musical origin of language. Maybe the solution is simple, like turning a right-hand glove inside out so that it fits on the left hand. A search for God in time and memory, I expect, will lead me to discover the musical origin of language.

"He believed, like Vico, that the world's first languages were in song," Bruce Chatwin says in *The Songlines,* speaking of a village schoolmaster he met in China. "Early man, he said, had learnt to speak by imitating the calls of animals and birds, and had lived in musical harmony with the rest of creation."[70] The songlines themselves described by Chatwin are another instance, being geographical lines across aboriginal Australia, each songline with its own guiding song, changing language in its thousand-mile progress across the land. An individual's first language, too, may be in song. One of my earliest memories is waking up in a playpen singing. My own experience of learning the names of things in childhood I describe in a song in my first song cycle,

My grandfather
would take me on a way
that later I would walk alone,
remembering a last
time I had passed a loved
red cedar and a mossyback along

the river running,
—I would stop and point
to see what he would call them,
and whatever he called anything,
that was its name.[71]

Saint Augustine talks about learning the names of things this way in his *Confessions,* and Wittgenstein begins his *Philosophical Investigations* quoting this passage from Augustine and criticizing it, saying this is like learning a language when you already know one, learning French, for instance, when you already know English. "And now, I think, we can say: Augustine describes the learning of human language as if the child came into a strange country and did not understand the language of the country, that is, as if it already had a language, only not this one."[72] Perhaps the child does have a language, I want to say, the nonverbal language of music. Maybe that is how human beings came to language in the first place, knowing the nonverbal language of music. It is true, the language of words cannot be deduced from the language of music, like the right–hand glove that cannot be fitted on the left hand unless it is turned inside out. Somehow that turning inside out will have occurred in the origin of language, if "the world's first languages were in song." How? As Wittgenstein goes on to say, "Or again: as if the child could already *think,* only not yet speak. And 'think' would here mean something like 'talk to itself'." Thinking in music, I want to suggest, where indeed "Thinking is thanking," is perhaps how we come to thinking in words, as if words were music inside out.

"Man possesses the capacity of constructing languages in which every sense can be expressed, without having an idea how and what each word means," Wittgenstein says, "—just as one speaks without knowing how the single sounds are produced."[73] This is truer of music than it is of words: we have the capacity of making music in which every sense can be expressed, without having an idea how and what each melody means. What then is the origin of music? Is there *a circle of words and music?* Apart from the calls of animals and birds, does human music have its origin in language just as language has its origin in music? I would guess that it does, that words and music are interdependent like the two hemispheres of the brain. The common element is rhythm, the rhythm of verse and the rhythm of music, and that common element finds expression in dance.

"And David danced before the Lord with all his might." That is what it means, I think, to love "with all your might," and there we have an eternal presence in the body. If we are searching then in time and memory, like Saint Augustine in his *Confessions,* searching for God, we come upon the musical origin of language and, I suppose, the linguistic origin of music, we come upon the circle of words and music, and we find God in our own "musical harmony with the rest of creation," as if to say, like the American composer John Adams, "the secret of grace is harmony."[74] Adams speaks of a vision or dream in which he saw Meister Eckhart with a child on his shoulder telling Eckhart the secret of grace, and the secret is harmony. That is what we find on the side of music, and on the other side, that of words, we find the stories of God, and there is a connection between the two if words are music inside out. The stories of God somehow reflect the secret of grace that is harmony. "Do you still remember God?" Rilke asks the Stranger in his *Stories of God,* and in the Stranger's eyes he can see long, shaded avenues leading back to what seems a point of light. "Yes," he answers, "I still remember God."[75] So there is a memory of God in our memory theatre, a memory in the form of stories on the side of words and a memory in the form of harmony on the side of music, and the stories are like the right hand of God in Rilke's stories and the harmony is like the left hand. In fact, the Stranger in that particular story seems to be the left hand of God. So the harmony is inside the stories, and the stories are the harmony inside out. But it is clear that all of this is image and symbol, and the memory theatre of our mind is a theatre of images and symbols, and the reality is the relationship with God that is being expressed in the harmony and in the stories.

"Why can't my right hand give my left hand money?"[76] Wittgenstein asks, to suggest the impossibility of a private language. Yet it is possible to set words to music, a real exchange between one side of me and the other.

> I will turn my mind to a parable,
> with the harp I will solve my problem,[77]

the psalmist sings. My problem may be a troubled body, a divided heart, a stifled cry. By turning my mind to a parable I give expression to my stifled cry, by setting words to music I solve with the harp the problem of my divided heart, and by dancing, though I have a dancer to dance my songs, I learn to love with my body, for "How can we know the dancer from the dance?"[78]

Our memory of God, then, on the musical side of the brain is harmony and that is the key to our memory on the verbal side in the stories of God, as in Dante's saying "his will is our peace" (*la sua voluntate e nostra pace*).[79] Matthew Arnold thought that was one of the greatest lines in poetry. It is true, musical harmony is an image of the inner harmony or inner peace we find in our soul's center. Harmony really is, though, "the secret of grace," as the composer John Adams says, and it leads in the stories of God to the story of an original harmony lost in our emergence and separation as a human race and our emergence and separation as individuals, and it leads to the hope of a final harmony to be regained in the end. And yet if "we all have within us a center of stillness surrounded by silence,"[80] it is something that exists now in a kingdom of God that is within us. It seems to go with our vision of a great circle of life and light and love that is "from God and of God and towards God."

My personal computer I am using at this moment is an external image of my brain as I am describing it, as a memory palace or a memory theatre with two hemispheres, one verbal and the other musical, for my computer is a Macintosh with two systems of software, Microsoft Word for words and Finale for music, and there is difficulty in trying to bring anything over from the one to the other, for instance to insert a page of music in among pages of words, that mirrors the difficulty in the brain of going from the one side to the other. But the computer, though it works with symbols, is far more literal-minded than the brain, and the human brain is much more suitable for the "poetic wisdom" of the mind.

I return now to the three questions with which I began to set out the riddle of eternal life:

> Am I my world?
> Am I my time?
> Am I my body?

I have been saying No, I am *in* my world, I am *in* my time, I am *in* my body, with the thought of thus leaving open the way to eternal life. Indwelling in my world, in my time, in my body, I pray with Saint Augustine,

> May I know me!
> May I know thee!

and I find the answer to my prayer in an *I and thou* relationship with God. I am who I am in relationship with God, and "God is spirit," as Jesus tells the woman at the well.

"I am my world," Wittgenstein's saying, as he indicates by writing beside it in parentheses "the microcosm," is not meant to be true of the universe, the macrocosm, but only of the little world, the microcosm, me as an epitome of the larger world. "Am I my time?" likewise, Heidegger's question at the end of his lecture on time, and Augustine's, who, as Heidegger says, "pursued the question so far as to ask whether spirit itself is time," is from the standpoint before self. And the popular book *Our Bodies Ourselves*,[81] where it is implied we are our bodies, is likewise from the standpoint before ourselves. It is not that the standpoint of the self is "fictional,"[82] as is said from a materialist point of view where the mind is equated with the brain, where instead of "I think therefore I am" we would have to say "The brain thinks and I am a fiction." Rather, self is relational, and by relating to myself, as Kierkegaard says, I am grounded transparently in God. So if we move on to the standpoint of an *I and thou* relationship with God, like Saint Augustine in his *Confessions*, then the world for us is the great world, the universe, and I am *in* the world, and I see myself in terms of a reality that is greater than myself, or as Alcoholics Anonymous always say "a power that is greater than ourselves," and it is in relation to that power greater than myself that I may hope for eternal life, so that death is not the end, as it would be if I were my time, which comes to an end, or if I were my body, which is mortal.

Is there a deeper life then that can survive death? Can *I and thou* with God survive death, and how can we know? By relating to myself and willing to be myself I am grounded transparently in God. That is Kierkegaard's formula for an *I and thou* with God and for an eternal consciousness. The knowing is in the transparency of the grounding. "I know whom I have believed,"[83] Saint Paul writes to Timothy, and that I think is what is meant by transparent grounding, a conscious trusting in God. I live in an *I and thou* with God, and "I know whom I have believed." Yet mere survival is not desirable. It will be eternal life only if it is life and light and love. "I know whom I have believed" is believing in the great circle of life and light and love, believing in going home to God. I think of the song "Going Home" on the theme of the slow movement of the New World Symphony, and I think of lines from Wordsworth's Ode "Intimations of Immortality,"

> Trailing clouds of glory do we come
> From God, who is our home.[84]

I realize there is an idea here of the pre-existence of souls, as in Plato and Virgil and in the early Christian theologian Origen.

Does the great circle of life and light and love imply pre-existence as well as life after death? Here we come back to Wittgenstein's questions, "Is a riddle solved by the fact that I survive for ever? Is this eternal life not as enigmatic as our present one?" and his answer, "The solution of the riddle of space and time lies *outside* space and time." My own answer is simply an *I and thou* relationship with God, and the conscious trust of "I know whom I have believed."

"Riddling, perplexed, labyrinthical soul!"

Poor intricated soul! Riddling,
perplexed, labyrinthical soul!

—John Donne

◆

If there is a riddle of eternal life, it is a riddle of the "riddling, perplexed, labyrinthical soul." The ten riddles in Tolkien's *Hobbit* are mountain, teeth, wind, sun on the daisies, dark, eggs, fish, fish on a little table—man at table sitting on a stool—the cat has the bones, time, and finally the Ring.[1] The nearest thing to eternal life is time, and time is seen there as devouring all things. If the body situates the soul, as I have been saying, does the complexity of the soul come from the body? And if the brain situates the mind, does the complexity of the mind come from the brain? "Where do mathematics come from?" George Lakoff and Rafael Nuñez have asked, and they find the answer in "embodied mind."[2]

"Poor intricated soul! Riddling, perplexed, labyrinthical soul!" John Donne exclaims in his sermon "terrifying the atheist."[3] Although he is speaking to the atheist, what he says seems good as a universal description of the human soul. The connection with atheism, nevertheless, is illuminating. I think of Kierkegaard's concept of the self as relational. The complexity of the soul is that of the self relating to itself. "I think therefore I am." It is I who think, and it is I who am. What is said of the soul is what is true of the self in its relation to itself and to others and to God. By relating to myself and willing to be myself I am grounded transparently in God. But if I do not relate to myself or if I am unwilling to be myself, the grounding in God is obscured. Thus atheism. The many forms of despair that Kierkegaard describes then are forms of disrelation of the self or of unrelatedness. If I am unwilling to be myself, if I am unaware of having an eternal self, if I will to be myself but it is will rather than willingness, the grounding in God is obscured.

Here then is a source of spiritual complexity, that self is relational. There is, first of all, the relation of self and soul, as in Yeats' poem "A Dialogue of Self and Soul,"⁴ an inner dialogue where the voice of self speaks for this life and this world and that of soul speaks for the life beyond and the otherworld. And there are "the three voices of poetry"⁵ described by T. S. Eliot, the solo voice of self or of self struggling, as he says, with an octopus or an angel, and there is secondly the voice of the One before the Many, as in ancient drama the one actor and the chorus, and there is lastly the manifold voice of the Many, as when the second actor was introduced in drama and there could be dialogue and interaction, or as Martin Buber says, *I and thou*. It is the manifold complexity then of relationship, the relation with self and with others, and the possibility finally of a great simplicity in an *I and thou* with God.

"Thou couldest not say that thou believest not in God, if there were no God," Donne argues with the atheist, and then he imagines different situations, a tragic play, a sermon, the day of judgement, the hour of death, tonight at midnight, and asks "Is there a God now?" But the complexity of soul he speaks of, where does it come from? There are two sources, I gather, embodiment and relationship. There is embodiment of mind and of soul expressed in metaphor, and there are the many voices of relationship. Let us consider these and ask "Is there a God now?"

"Embodied in the mystery of words"

I think, first of all, of some lines from Wordsworth's *Prelude,*

> Visionary power
> Attends the motions of the viewless winds,
> Embodied in the mystery of words.[6]

Wordsworth is telling in *The Prelude* the story of his own life, "The Growth of a Poet's Mind," as he also calls it, and in this part he is telling of his reading, especially of great poetry. What is "the mystery of words"? It is metaphor, I think, if we take metaphor in its full scope. Nowadays "cognitive science" is about "conceptual metaphors," relating everyday language to science and mathematics, but I want to consider metaphor also in religion and even in magic. Science, I am thinking, relates the human body to the body of the world; magic relates the human soul to the soul of the world; and religion relates the body to the soul.

Metaphor (*metaphora* in Greek) is a term in Aristotle's *Poetics,* defined as one thing for another, and thought of as including analogy. Although he thinks of metaphor as a figure of speech, Aristotle thinks "poetry is more philosophical and more serious than history," for "poetry tends to express universals, and history particulars."[7] Nowadays metaphor in cognitive science is held to be more than just a figure of speech, and "metaphorical mappings are systematic and not arbitrary."[8] I wonder if this can be said not only of science but also of religion, if it can be said of those three basic metaphors in the Gospel of John, life and light and love, and of the great circle of life and light and love I have been describing where "The love is from God and of God and towards God." What then of magic and a vision like that of Yeats of the human soul (*anima hominis*) and the soul of the world (*anima mundi*)?

If we look more closely at these metaphors, the body of the world, the soul of the world, and at the relation of body and soul, two sayings of Wittgenstein come to mind. One we have already quoted, an early saying, "I am my world (the microcosm)," and the other a late saying, "The human body is the best picture of the human soul."⁹ What we have here are two images, the microcosm an image of the macrocosm, and the human body an image of the human soul. If knowing is not simply imaging but insight into image, then knowing the macrocosm is not simply imaging it but insight into the microcosm which is its image, and knowing the soul is insight into the image that is the human body. Yet what is insight? It is understanding the relation, I gather, here the relation of microcosm and macrocosm and that of body and soul.

We seek these insights then "embodied in the mystery of words." If the mystery of words is metaphor, the basic metaphor, it seems, is the human body. Yet the body is mortal,

> I have a sin of fear, that when I have spun
> My last thread, I shall perish on the shore;
> Swear by thyself, that at my death thy Sun
> Shall shine as it shines now, and heretofore.¹⁰

Is body a conceptual metaphor? Is the human body a conceptual metaphor of the body of the world, and is this the basic conceptual metaphor of science? Is body also a conceptual metaphor of soul, and is this the basic conceptual metaphor of religion?

If the human body is a conceptual metaphor, it points beyond its own mortality, imaging the world and imaging the soul, as "metaphorical mappings are systematic and not arbitrary." Imaging the world, I see myself participating in all humanity. Imaging the soul, I see hope of eternal life. "I have a sin of fear . . ." are words from "A Hymn to God the Father," and so are from a standpoint before God. All three come together, God and world and soul, in Donne's meditations at this point in his life, his *memento mori*,

> No man is an island,
> entire of itself;

every man is a piece of the continent,
a part of the main.
If a clod be washed away by the sea,
Europe is the less,
as well as if a promontory were,
as well as if a manor of thy friend's
or of thine own were:
any man's death diminishes me,
because I am involved in mankind,
and therefore never send to know
for whom the bell tolls;
it tolls for thee.[11]

Imaging the world, the anatomy of the human body images an anatomy of the world, and that is the title of one of Donne's longest poems, "An Anatomy of the World." Mortality, though, seems to govern the image, for he is commemorating there the death of Elizabeth Drury. It is the study of the human body in Renaissance art, Leonardo and Michelangelo, that leads to the body becoming a conceptual metaphor. *Anatomia* means "dissection." "All we know," William Harvey says in the dedication of his treatise on the circulation of the blood, "is still infinitely less than all that still remains unknown."[12] Nowadays the focus has shifted from heart to brain, and in cognitive science the world is seen in terms of the embodied mind. The brain, and the body generally, is seen in terms of evolutionary and molecular biology, as in the human genome project seeking to count and classify the genes.

Imaging the soul, on the other hand, is the subject of Donne's other long poem, "Of the Progress of the Soul," the sequel to "An Anatomy of the World." The soul's progress, its journey after death, is inevitably described in bodily terms, here as in Dante's descriptions of hell and purgatory and heaven. If "the human body is the best picture of the human soul," it is the best picture of the soul even after death, not the body after death, to be sure, but the body in life. That is why there is doubt, why

> I have a sin of fear, that when I have spun
> My last thread, I shall perish on the shore.

And that is why there has to be an appeal to God, to a power that is greater than ourselves,

> Swear by thyself, that at my death thy Sun
> Shall shine as it shines now, and heretofore;
> And, having done that, thou has done,
> I fear no more.

It is this greater reality, nevertheless, eternal life with the God of the living, that the body seems to call for, imaging the world and imaging the soul. The human body, as Charles Williams says in his essay "The Index of the Body," is the index of a greater reality, "a whole being significant of a greater whole."[13] But what is that greater whole? Actually the body is a double index, I believe, an image of the soul and also of the world, and this is what leads to the idea of a world soul. There are really three metaphors here, the body imaging the world and the body imaging the soul and the fusion of the two metaphors in that of the world soul. What we need to seek now is *insight into image.* What is the relation of the human body and the body of the world in science? What is the relation of body and soul in religion? And what is the relation of the human soul and the world soul in magic?

What if this present were the world's last night?[14]

It is the mortality of my body that would make it for me the world's last night. The relation of the human body to the world, I want to say, is that of situating and being situated. "Everything that exists is situated," Max Jacob's saying, "Everything that is above matter is situated; matter itself is situated," goes also for the human body, but I want to add that matter situates, that the human body situates. What does it situate? Well, the soul, but speaking of science we can say it situates our observations. The human body is situated in the world, but it also situates our observations of the world. Although the situation of the observer does not matter, according to the principle of relativity, in uniform relative motion, the presence of the observer, according to the uncertainty principle, affects what is happening on the very small scale. We are both observers and players, as Shakespeare said, on the stage of the world.

All this throws light on evolution and the evolution of the human body. If we see matter as having not only a passive but also an active role, not only as situated but also as situating, we can see evolution as purposive. And if we see the human body too as having not only a passive but also an active role, not only as situated in the world but also as situating our observations of the world, we can see language not merely as a "spandrel,"[15] a corner created by an arch, a by-product of human evolution, but as belonging to its purpose. Chance, I believe, is a name for our unknowing. There are two elements in poetry, Max Jacob goes on to say, "style or will and situation or emotion,"[16] situating, we could say, and being situated, and so too, I gather, in the evolution of language. "Situation or emotion" is there in our experience of the world, and "style or will" develops to situate our experience.

"Embodied in the mystery of words," as Wordsworth says, the "visionary power" of the soul "attends the motions of the viewless winds." That visionary power appears in the great religions, in Judaism and Christianity and Islam, embodied in the words of their teachings, in the Torah, in the Gospel, in the Koran. In Christianity it is embodied in the Gospel in the mystery of the Word made flesh. If body and soul are related in this way, as I have been saying, that body situates soul, what is happening in "the mystery of words" in the great religions is a situating of the visionary power of the soul. That visionary power gets situated in a people in Judaism, in a person in Christianity, in a scripture in Islam. This situating has an effect in each of these religions. There is a relating of persons to the person of Christ in Christianity. He takes our place ("substitutionary atonement"), or instead, as I believe, we take his place, entering into his relationship with God, "my Father and your Father," as he says to Mary Magdalene, "my God and your God."

"Visionary power," as Wordsworth says, "attends the motions of the viewless winds." In Christianity "The wind blows where it wills," as Jesus says to Nicodemus, "and you hear the sound of it, but you do not know whence it comes or whither it goes."[17] There, I believe, he is alluding to the great circle of life and light and love, coming from God and going to God. It is God who is unknown. That is why "you do not know whence it comes or whither it goes." God is unknown (we do not know what God is, as Saint Thomas Aquinas says),[18] but we know the relationship with God, the *I and thou* with God. The metaphor of life and light and love, and the great circle coming from God and going to God, I want to say, is "a conceptual metaphor" where "metaphorical mappings are systematic and not arbitrary." Here is the vision of the "visionary power" of the soul, attending "the motions of the viewless winds," and "embodied in the mystery of words,"

> I saw Eternity the other night,
> Like a great ring of pure and endless light,
> All calm, as it was bright.

What then of a vision like that of Yeats, relating the human soul to the soul of the world? Here again, I believe, we have a metaphor, actually a fusion of two metaphors, that of the human body as image of the world and that of the human body as image of the soul, but the body has dropped out of the metaphor and all that is left is the soul and the world soul. Is there then a soul of the world? "I came to believe in a Great Memory passing on from generation to generation,"[19] Yeats says, and that is what he seems to mean by the world soul. Personal memory belongs to the human soul (*anima hominis*), according to Yeats, and the Great Memory belongs to the soul of the world (*anima mundi*). Is there then "a Great Memory passing on from generation to generation"? Nicolas

Cusanus, writing during the Renaissance, speaks of the world soul, according to the Platonic tradition, containing the forms or archetypes of all things. Nicolas, though, wants to find the forms or archetypes rather in the Word, according to the Gospel of John. I have turned those opening words of the Gospel into a song:

> In the beginning was the Word,
> and the Word was with God,
> and the Word was God.
> This was in the beginning with God;
> all came to be through this,
> and without this nothing came
> that ever came to be.
> In this was life,
> and the life was the light of humankind,
> and the light shines in the darkness,
> and the darkness has not overshadowed it.[20]

Here is "the mystery of words" in the metaphor of the Word. Here too, I want to say, is "a conceptual metaphor" where "metaphorical mappings are systematic and not arbitrary." I have found a further development of this metaphor at the end of Hermann Broch's *Death of Virgil,* "it was the word beyond speech."[21] As "in the beginning was the Word" so, according to this, "in the end was the Word." As Broch describes it, this is a deathbed experience, but there is an intimation of eternal life in it, a beatific vision in which all is seen in the Word. Here again eternal life is something that begins already on this side of death, and death is seen as an eternal return,

> In my beginning is my end;
> In my end is my beginning.

My beginning is in the Word, and my end is in "the word beyond speech" that is the same Word that was in the beginning, or that is my hope, that "the word beyond speech" at the end of my life will be none other than the Word that was in the beginning. There is a hint of this already in Yeats' vision, insofar as "a Great Memory" involves thinking back to the beginning. I think of Saint Augustine in his *Confessions* thinking back to the beginning of his life in infancy but then in the later books meditating on memory and time and the beginning of time, as if he were thinking back to the beginning of time and to the Word that was in the beginning.

Thinking back to the Word in the beginning, "I summon up the remembrance of things past," and thinking forward to the Word at the end, with "the prophetic soul of the wide world," as Shakespeare says in his Sonnets, I am "dreaming on things to come."[22] So thinking in this great circle of life and light and love, coming from God and going to God, I am thinking in harmony with the soul of the world. Of the figure of Wisdom it is said "in every generation she passes into holy souls and makes them friends of God and prophets."[23] That is close to the image of "a Great Memory passing on from generation to generation." Indeed the metaphor of a world soul seems to correspond to that of a great circle of life and light and love, coming from God and going to God, beginning and ending in the Word, going from "remembrance of things past" to "dreaming on things to come." And the relation of the human soul to the world soul is that of personal memory to "a Great Memory," that of a life story to the larger story of the world, like Saint Augustine going from his own story to that of Genesis.

What then is the relation of a life story to the larger story of the world? According to Saint Augustine's thinking, "the story of the soul wandering away from God and then in torment and tears finding its way home through conversion is also the story of the entire created order,"[24] his own story is the story of the world. This is a version of the great circle coming from God and going to God, where the farthest point from God on the circle is not merely loneliness but sin. "Loneliness is not the sickness unto death," Dag Hammarskjöld writes in his diary just before his great turning point where he says "Thanks!" and "Yes!"[25] If sin, or the sickness unto death, is separation from God, from others, from oneself, loneliness is an awareness of the separation, of the disrelation or the unrelatedness, and so is a step towards reunion, towards "Thanks!" and "Yes!" "Thinking is thanking" then, the mystic saying, is the key to thinking back on the great circle to the beginning/ending.

So in "the mystery of words" there are five things to consider, as Plato says in his Seventh Letter: naming, expressing, imaging, knowing, and being.[26] His example is simply a circle, but ours shall be the great circle of life and light and love we have been contemplating. Naming (*onoma*)—"My name and yours," Ursula LeGuin says, "and the true name of the sun, or a spring of water, or an unborn child, all are syllables of the great word that is very slowly spoken by the shining of the stars."[27] Expressing (*logos*)—this is "the great word," the Word in the beginning and in the end, the Logos in the Gospel of John. Imaging (*eidolon*)—this is the story of coming from God and returning to God, the metaphor of a great circle of life and light and love. Knowing (*episteme*)—"We can know more than we can tell" (Polanyi), for we can tell the story of coming from God and returning to God, but we can know the relationship with God. Being (*on*)—the *I and thou* relationship with God, "I in them and thou in me"[28] as is said in the Gospel of John.

"Thanks!" and "Yes!" is enhanced by "I came to believe in a Great Memory passing on from generation to generation," Yeats' saying, and Shakespeare's, "the prophetic soul of the wide world dreaming on things to come." The world soul enhances the metaphor of the human body imaging the soul and imaging the world. If science then relates the human body to the body of the world, and magic relates the human soul to the soul of the world, and religion relates the body to the soul, there is a convergence in "Thanks!" and "Yes!" affirming the great circle of life and light and love.

"Is there a God now?" Donne's question, finds its answer in "Thanks!" and "Yes!" and generally in "Thinking is thanking," as if thinking were carried on in the presence of God. Thinking is "embodied in the mystery of words," thanking in that of music, but as I was saying before, speaking of the right hand and the left hand, it is as if music were words inside out. And so too with thinking and thanking, it is as if thanking were thinking inside out, and "Song is the leap of mind in the eternal breaking out into sound."[29]

"The secret of grace is harmony"

It is in his preface to the Psalms that Saint Thomas Aquinas says "Song is the leap of mind in the eternal breaking out into sound." So you wonder if this is true of all song or only of sacred song like the Psalms or like the hymns he himself wrote to celebrate the Body of Christ. We have been speaking of the human body as an image of the soul and an image of the world. Here in these Eucharistic hymns the human body of Christ is an image of transcendence,

> *Pange, lingua, gloriosi*
> *Corporis mysterium.*

"Sing, my tongue, the mystery of the glorious Body."[30] Saint Thomas sings the risen body of Christ present under the appearances of bread and wine. I composed a Eucharistic song myself, based on the *Ave Verum* and playing on the words "alone" and "all one,"

> All one
> with us
> in body birth,
> All one
> with us alone
> in suffering,
> Alone

with us all one
in dying,
Be with us
then when
we are alone,
Jesus
with us
in body and in blood.[31]

My song is of God-with-us, Christ as Emmanuel, as I think of us
entering into his *I and thou* relationship with God.

An image of transcendence then, the human body of Christ
becomes an object of worship, as in the *Ave Verum* set to music by
Mozart in the last summer of his life,

> *Ave verum corpus natum de Maria Virgine*
> Hail true body born of Mary Virgin,
> *Vere passum immolatum in cruce pro homine,*
> Suffered truly, immolated on the cross for humankind,
> *Cujus latus perforatum unda fluxit et sanguine:*
> Whose side pierced flowed with water and with blood:
> *Esto nobis praegustatum in mortis examine.*
> Be unto us a foretaste in the passage of our death.[32]

As I listen to Mozart's music, I realize *the secret of grace is harmony.* That is what I hear in Mozart's music, grace and harmony,
grace as harmony. Putting words to this, I am thinking of a dream
the American composer John Adams had of Meister Eckhart with
a child on his shoulder whispering to him the secret of grace, and
the secret is harmony.[33]

Musical harmony conveys spiritual harmony. "It is the spirit
that gives life, the flesh is of no avail," Jesus says in the Gospel of
John after his discourse on the bread of life; "the words that I have
spoken to you are spirit and life."[34] All the same, it is the human

body of Christ, according to Christian belief, that conveys spirit and life, and so it is too that musical harmony conveys spiritual harmony, as in the prologue of the Epistle of John,

> What was from the beginning,
> what we have heard,
> what we have seen with our eyes,
> what we have looked upon,
> and our hands have handled,
> of the Word of life . . .[35]

There are the songs of time and the songs of eternity, but time is "a changing image of eternity," and so the songs of time too can convey the sense of eternity.

"Song is the leap of mind in the eternal breaking out into sound," therefore, is true not only of sacred song but of all song where musical harmony conveys spiritual harmony. Let us consider then the voices that are heard in music. Let us consider "the leap of mind (*exultatio mentis*) in the eternal (*de aeternis habita*) breaking out into sound (*prorumpens in vocem*)."

There are four memories, Yeats says in *A Vision*, the memory of the events of life, the memory of past lives, the memory of ideas, and the memory of "moments of exaltation."[36] The events of life are personal memory; the others, the past, the ideas, the moments of exaltation, are "a Great Memory." All of them, it seems, are voices in music, and the moments of exaltation become "the leap of mind" (*exultatio mentis*) that Saint Thomas describes. I can see the memories in the voices of music, for instance in Stravinsky's *Symphony of Psalms*, the memory of events in his setting of "Hear my prayer, O Lord . . ." and "Waiting, I waited on the Lord . . . ," the moments of exaltation in his setting of "Laudate" and "Alleluia," or in Górecki's *Symphony of Sorrowful Songs*, the memory of the past in the sorrowful songs, the moment of exaltation in his setting of the words of an eighteen-year-old girl on a cell wall of a Gestapo prison, "Little mother, do not cry . . . Hail Mary!" or in John

Adams' *Harmonium*, the memory of ideas of love and death in his setting of poems by John Donne and Emily Dickinson.[37] All of the memories, I can see, of life events, of the past, of ideas are transformed into moments of exaltation in music.

I can see here the design of a memory theatre, two hemispheres: words and music, and four memories in each hemisphere: the inner circle of personal memory, and then the outer circles of the past, of ideas, and of moments of exaltation. In one hemisphere these are the voices of poetry, in the other they are the voices of music. There is an overlap, though, between hemispheres, between words and music, a music of words. It is true, there are "songs without words," as Mendelssohn called them, but the guiding songs of a life are songs with words. I usually start from words when I am composing music. It is the rhythm of the words that guides me to the melody and it is the melody that guides me to the harmony. "The leap of mind" (*exultatio mentis*), the first element of song, is already there in the words and their rhythm, and this, the rhythm of the words, was called *musica* in ancient times, as for instance in Saint Augustine's unfinished work *De Musica*.

Psalms are the guiding songs in the *Confessions* of Saint Augustine, and especially Psalm 4 on the mind being illumined by God ("Lift up the light of thy countenance upon us, O Lord!"), Psalm 42 on the soul thirsting for God ("As a hart longs for flowing streams, so longs my soul for thee, O God"), and Psalm 139 on the human being known through and through by God ("O Lord, thou hast searched me and known me"). My own guiding song is especially Psalm 23 on being guided and guarded by God ("The Lord is my shepherd, I shall not want . . . I fear no evil . . . I shall dwell in the house of the Lord for ever"), as in my song reproduced above in "The Riddle of Eternal Life." I have written a song cycle called *The Voyage of Life* following on a memoir, *A Journey with God in Time*, and trying to cast my own life into the form of prayer as Saint Augustine does in his *Confessions*. Here then is personal memory in song form. Cast into the form of prayer, moreover, it does become "the leap of mind in the eternal breaking out into sound."

A guiding song thus is one that turns the truth of a life into music. I think again of Goethe's method of turning the truth of a life into poetry and of Saint Augustine's method of turning the truth of a life into prayer. There is "remembrance of things past" here and there is "dreaming on things to come." As an example I think of Newman's song "Lead Kindly Light," written off Sicily after he recovered from a near mortal bout with fever,

> Lead, kindly light
> amid the encircling gloom,
> lead thou me on;
> the night is dark,
> and I am far from home,
> lead thou me on.
> Keep thou my feet;
> I do not ask to see
> the distant scene;
> one step enough for me.[38]

These words come out of a crisis of life, and at the same time they are words of guard and guiding, and their guidance is to one step at a time out of the heart. I recited the song once at a retreat for Presbyterian ministers in western Illinois, and I told them I had never heard it sung. So they sang it for me, moving and beautiful. Also I gave it to a Jewish friend who recites it now every day.

"A Great Memory" too, as Yeats called it, "passing on from generation to generation," is passed on by way of songs, I believe. You wonder if there has been a loss of memory in our literate and technical civilization. All the same, we are in possession of the epics of war and journey in literary form, though we know they were originally sung. *War Music* is the suggestive title of a free translation of Homer by Christopher Logue.[39] For myself it was reading Homer's *Iliad* and Tolstoy's *War and Peace* forty years ago that led me to pacifism and what I now call "an unviolent way of life." War music then led me away from violence to peace, though

I realize too, as Gandhi discovered, there is nothing more difficult than peace. (I am writing this only a week after the terrorism in New York and Washington.) Here again "the secret of grace is harmony" or *the secret of harmony is grace.*

Living in peace, I have come to believe, is like living in the quiet eye of a storm, a moving hurricane, and so it means going on a journey full of adventures like the *Odyssey,* and like it a homecoming, and I have come to think of the human spirit as a homing spirit. The songs in "a Great Memory" are the epics of war and journey, but the epic of journey as a homecoming implies also the story of creation. Saint Augustine thinks back to the beginning of time and for him "the story of the soul wandering away from God and then in torment and tears finding its way home through conversion is the story of the entire created order." For me "a Great Memory" is essentially a memory of the great circle of life and light and love coming from God and returning to God. War is something that occurs at the point of greatest distance from God on the circle. It comes of our separation from God and from others and from ourselves.

"I sing of arms and the man," Virgil begins, combining war and journey in his epic, and past lives are a memory, according to his belief in reincarnation, but illustrious lives belong to "a Great Memory" even apart from such a belief, for instance Shakespeare's sources in lives and times. Kierkegaard imagines a thought experiment of reading the Gospels and reading Shakespeare's plays side by side and, he says, you will "shrink from the collisions."[40] I imagine the musical equivalent of the lives are *The Songlines,* as Bruce Chatwin calls them, pathways across aboriginal Australia each with its own guiding song, the Dreaming Tracks as the aboriginal people call them, the tracks of the ancestors, that is, and the Way of the Law.[41] Adopting this metaphor, I have composed *Songlines of the Gospel,* a song and dance cycle based on the Gospel of John.[42]

Reading the Gospel and reading Shakespeare side by side, Kierkegaard's thought experiment, I do "shrink from the collisions," but casting the Gospel into Songlines or really into song and dance, I thought again of the words "David danced before the Lord with all his might," and I thought I was learning what it is to love "with all your might." My friend the composer Michael Rose, seeing the videotape we made of *Songlines of the Gospel,* loved especially the ending when the video camera was showing one of the dancers, Anne Geary, dancing with a very serious expression on her face and then at the end, realizing it was over, she smiled. Michael thought this was the wonderful moment of "return to ordinary life." Here again there is the collision, as between the Gospels and Shakespeare's plays, but the collision has turned into a return from the Gospel to ordinary life.

Returning to ordinary life, though, can be like Don Quixote returning from the Cave of Montesinos, where he has learned, as in Plato's allegory of the cave, that what we take for reality is only shadow. It is the memory of ideas then that is of reality, according to Plato's vision, and also according to Saint Augustine in his unfinished work *De Musica,* where he goes from changing to unchanging numbers. I wrote a song called "Unchanging Number" to Saint Augustine on reading his *De Musica,*

Tell me, Master,
how you turn
from changing to unchanging number
and are sensible to
music of eternal life,
or tell me rather how to listen
to unchanging number in the changing
and to hear eternal music
in the song of earth.[43]

Soul and music are akin, Plato says in his dialogue *Timaeus,* where he also says time is "a changing image of eternity." "All the diverse emotions of our spirit have their various modes in voice and chant appropriate in each case," Saint Augustine says in his

Confessions, "and are stirred by a mysterious inner kinship."[44] Our many feelings then find expression in a changing image that is time, and insight into the image that time is reveals the unchanging reality that eternity is. Music is of time, according to this way of thinking, and is "a changing image of eternity," and eternal music is that unchanging reality that is being imaged by time. To realize this is "to listen to unchanging number in the changing and to hear eternal music in the song of earth."

Moments of exaltation, I gather, are moments when we "hear eternal music in the song of earth." I think of Tolkien's song cycle, *The Road Goes Ever On,* songs of Middle-earth but with a hint of eternity, as in the title song, "The Road Goes Ever On." I mention this song cycle mainly because it has been an inspiration to me to write song cycles of my own, scoring them simply for voice and piano and leaving all matters of choreography to the dancers. My first song cycle was especially important to me, *Ayasofya,* though it was purely a song cycle and not yet a song and dance cycle like my later ones, important because it represented my return to music, my "road not taken," after years of following my "road taken," the way of words. And the title song is melismatic, simply my name for the figure of Holy Wisdom, from the Turkish *Ayasofya* for the Greek *Hagia Sophia,* a church for a thousand years and then a mosque for five hundred years and now an empty monument.

"Ayasofya," the title song, is truly for me "the leap of mind in the eternal breaking out into sound." The melody is one I thought of years ago, when I was a teenager, and had originally intended for a Kyrie in a Mass:[45]

Now I have cast it into a form like that of Bach's Prelude in C, the opening piece of his *Well-Tempered Clavier*. There are no words except the name Ayasofya, divided into two, Aya-sofya, and repeated through all the harmonic changes by a soprano, ranging through the entire soprano range from middle C to high A. My sopranos, singing subsequent song cycles, have used it for a warm-up, because it covers the entire range and is easy to sing with its open vowels.

I can see now that I have designed a memory theatre with two hemispheres, words and music, I have to reject the materialism that underlies much of cognitive neuroscience. Matter for me is situated in space and time but also situates, the brain situates the mind, the body situates the soul. A memory theatre is about situating. I have used the cognitivist idea of a "conceptual metaphor," it is true, where "metaphorical mappings are systematic and not arbitrary." The basic metaphor is the human body, an image of the soul, an image of the world, and in Eucharist even an image of transcendence. Knowing, though, for me is not simply imaging but insight into image, and insight into image is understanding relationship. "We can know more than we can tell," and while story and metaphor we can tell, relationship we can know, *I and thou* and ultimately *I and thou* with God.

Spirit is relatedness, *I and thou*, or in the Gospel of John, "I in them and thou in me," indwelling and relatedness. There are the things of life and there is our relation to the things of life. The things are the situations and the persons of the life; the relation is the life of the spirit and is essentially twofold, knowledge and love, knowledge taking things in and love going out to things. The things of life enter and pass; the life of the spirit abides, or that is the hope of eternal life, the hope that the life of the spirit can endure and survive the death of our bodies and the passing of the things of our life. Everything depends on this, that we do not simply live and die but we always have a relationship to our life and to our death. It is our relationship with God, *I and thou* with God then, that is eternal life already begun and the hope of life ever after.

There is method in this hope, moreover, Goethe's method of turning the truth of a life into poetry and Saint Augustine's method of turning the truth of a life into prayer. Goethe turns the truth of his life into the poetry of *Faust* and ends in hope, *Das Ewigweibliche zieht uns hinan*, "the eternal womanly leads us on."[46] When he says "the eternal womanly," I think of my Ayasofya, the figure of Holy Wisdom. Saint Augustine turns the truth of his life into prayer and he too ends in hope, the sabbath rest of eternal life, as if to say we are still in the Sixth Day of the Genesis, when God is creating human beings, and the Seventh Day, when we rest and God rests, is still to come. Turning the truth of my own life into the poetry and music of song and dance cycles, I am learning what it is to love "with all your heart, and with all your soul, and with all your might." So I am learning what Saint Augustine means when he begins by saying "our heart is restless until it rests in you."

He ends by praying "Lord God, grant us peace; for you have given us all things, the peace of quietness, the peace of the sabbath, a peace with no evening."[47] Living in peace, I can see, especially living in peace at this time, just a few days after the terrorism in New York and Washington, is like living in the quiet eye of a storm, a moving hurricane, and we have to keep moving to stay in the eye, our center of stillness surrounded by the silence of God's presence.

"Tell me where all past years are"

Go, and catch a falling star,
Get with child a mandrake root,
Tell me, where all past years are,
Or who cleft the Devil's foot.

— John Donne

◆ A memory theatre I have then with two hemispheres, words and music, but there is a mystery of memory. To tell where all past years are is like catching a falling star or getting with child a mandrake root or telling who cleft the devil's foot. One answer is to say, like Kurt Gödel, there is no objective lapse of time. Another is to say the past no longer exists, the future does not yet exist, and only the present exists, time does lapse and continues to exist only in memory, but then this existence in memory is mysterious, as Saint Augustine found searching for God in time and memory.

There is personal memory and there is "a Great Memory," as Yeats said, "passing on from generation to generation."[1] If I search for God in time and memory, like Saint Augustine, I am searching for a personal memory of God in my own life and I am searching for "a Great Memory" of God, "passing on from generation to generation." Is there such a thing as a personal memory or a Great Memory of God? Taking the Gospels and especially the Gospel of John as my guide, I believe "God is spirit" and God acts spiritually, kindling the heart and illumining the mind. So I search for the illumining of the mind and the kindling of the heart in the memory of my own life and in the memory passing on from generation to generation. That means not taking everything that happens or that has happened in human memory to be the will of God—the common notion of God—but only the kindling of the heart and the illumining of the mind. So if I ask myself Rilke's question "Do you still remember God?" and I answer like Rilke's Stranger "Yes, I still remember God,"[2] what I am remembering is the illumining and the kindling.

"Take this ring, Master," Cirdan says to Gandalf in Tolkien's epic, "for your labours will be heavy; but it will support you in the weariness that you have taken upon yourself. For this is the Ring of Fire, and with it you may rekindle hearts in a world that grows chill."[3] Well, this is how I see God working in the world, God who is spirit, acting spiritually, illumining minds and kindling hearts, rekindling hearts in a world that grows chill. It is "a world that grows chill," sin is at work in the world, the mystery of iniquity, the mystery of lovelessness, and God is working against the growing chill, against the lovelessness, kindling and rekindling hearts, illumining minds, and we too can rekindle hearts, like Gandalf in Tolkien's story, we can work with God, seeing and saying and doing what God is doing. By seeing the kindling and the illumining, and by saying it as I am here, I am also doing it.

To remember the kindling of the heart and the illumining of the mind is a matter of discerning spiritual influences. There are classical "rules for the discernment of spirits,"[4] for instance in *The Spiritual Exercises of Saint Ignatius*. Let us see what it would be to discern spiritual influences in personal memory and in "a Great Memory passing on from generation to generation."

A Personal Memory of God

Consolation and desolation are the principal signs of spiritual influence in those classical rules of discernment, in particular "consolation without a cause,"[5] consolation coming from within the person without an external cause such as a call or a letter from a friend, consolation coming, I would say, from the kindling of the heart and the illumining of the mind. My own understanding of the kindling and the illumining is to see the kindling of the heart as fundamental and as leading to the illumining of the mind. So for instance when I am trying to discern my own path in life, which way to go, I have to wait on insight, to wait for the kindling of my heart, and that leads to the illumining of my mind, to seeing the way. And when it comes to deciding the way, the criterion for me is the peace, that there is peace on the true way, as in Dante's saying "his will is our peace" (*la sua voluntate e nostra pace*), the will of God can be discerned in the inner peace. What this implies is that we do not simply choose our way in life, choose our lifework, choose our life partner, "choose our essence,"[6] as Sartre said, but we discover our way, discover our heart's desire.

"We all have within us a center of stillness surrounded by silence,"[7] Dag Hammarskjöld's opening statement for the Meditation Room at the UN, describes the locus of this kindling and illumining. It is by entering into my center of stillness that I wait on the kindling of my heart and the illumining of my mind. I take the surrounding silence to be the presence of God. When I am in my center of stillness, I am dwelling in peace and it is there in the peace that I can discern my way in life. When I am outside my center, outside my peace, living in fear or in sadness, it is as though I were outside my heart, certainly outside my heart's desire. "When the heart casts a shadow instead of dancing light," Patricia McKillip says, "there story begins."[8]

If I were to write my own *Stories of God,* like Rilke's, I would have to begin there, where "the heart casts a shadow instead of dancing light." For me the shadow is loneliness. Rilke begins with "The Tale of the Two Hands of God," and I immediately think of Lessing's saying, "If God held all truth in his right hand and the lifelong pursuit of it in his left, I would choose the left."[9] Loneliness for me goes with the lifelong pursuit of truth, the longing in loneliness, the longing to be unalone, the longing ultimately to be "alone with the Alone." To say, for instance, "we read to know that we are not alone"[10] suggests the link between the lifelong pursuit of truth and the longing in loneliness to be unalone. Reading has been my way of pursuing truth, and I do read to know that I am not alone. My own left hand (and right brain), though, I connect with music, and my own right hand (and left brain) I connect with words. Maybe all truth and the lifelong pursuit of truth are like words and music, and maybe the one is the other inside out.

It is in his second story, "The Stranger," that Rilke asks the question "Do you still remember God?" and the Stranger, it seems, is the left hand of God. For me the story of the two hands is that of words and music, and it is a surprise to me to connect words with all truth and music with the lifelong pursuit of truth, but I do see the symbolic connection of words with the Word and of music with the Spirit and with God illumining the mind through words and kindling the heart through music (the heart can be kindled also by the music of words). Lessing's own conclusion that "the aspiration to truth is more precious than its assured possession"[11] goes with his choosing the left hand over the right. My own experience of being right-handed and following the way of words as my road taken and treating the way of music as my "road not taken" seems to reflect an equal and opposite alternative, my choosing the right hand over the left. All the same, I come in the end to the experience of the road not taken rejoining the road taken, of music rejoining words in my song and dance cycles.

My conception of God then has been the God of Jesus, "my Father and your Father," as he says to Mary Magdalene, "my God and your God," the God who is spirit, the God of the Gospel of John, and so God revealed by the Word and by "the words of eternal life." I know, though, "Nothing exists without music," as Isidore of Seville says, "for the universe itself is said to have been framed by a kind of harmony of sounds and the heaven itself revolves under the tones of that harmony."[12] When Tolkien and C. S. Lewis tell the story of creation, they both have it that God creates the world by singing, as if to say "In the beginning is the song."[13] Bringing words and music together then, I compose song cycles or song and dance cycles to echo the Word which is song in the beginning. Rilke's third story, "Why God Wants Poor People," is about God wanting to see human beings in their naked humanity. For me that humanity appears not in poverty so much as in song and dance.

God in disguise is the theme of Rilke's next three stories, his Russian tales, and they are all about song, even the first one, for it was a *bylina,* as he says, a folk epic that was sung, a story of Ivan the Terrible meeting God in disguise and learning from him the answer to three riddles. Rilke doesn't say what the riddles were, but Tolstoy says they were "how to know the proper moment for every deed, how to know which were the most essential people, and how not to err in deciding which pursuits were of the greatest importance," and the answers were "Now" and "he with whom you are" and "to do good to him."[14] This tale lived in people's hearts for centuries, Rilke says, when it was sung, until it died and was buried in books. "But were people so quiet that songs could sleep in their hearts?" he is asked. "They must have been," he answers. "It is said they spoke less, danced dances of slowly growing intensity that had something soothing in their sway, and above all, they did not laugh loudly, as one not infrequently hears them do today, despite our general high state of culture."[15]

I think again of Chaucer's advice, "Flee fro the prees, and dwelle with sothfastnesse." But why did the song die? Because "the words people use now, those heavy words one cannot sing, were its enemies and took from it one mouth after another." Rilke's second Russian tale then was "How Old Timofei Died Singing." It is like the Parable of the Prodigal Son, the son who goes away and comes back to his father, and I suppose God, not mentioned here, is like the father in the parable, and the father dies singing because his son has returned. God not mentioned here, I guess, is God in disguise as the old father who sings. I think of my grandfather who used to tell stories on our front porch on summer nights when I was a child and who used to take me on walks and answer my questions, telling me the names of things. I don't remember the stories but only how he used to tell them, but I suppose they are lodged in the back of my mind and they influence all I think and say and do.

A third and last Russian tale, "The Song of Justice," is also about song, an old blind man who sings a song of justice and stirs all hearts to throw off the oppression of the Polish Pans, and "the old man was God."[16] He was God in disguise, "and I didn't know," the storyteller says in surprise. That is how I think of God too, God as spirit, acting spiritually, illumining minds and kindling hearts, rekindling hearts "in a world that grows chill," a world that grows loveless and soulless. I see now why I have been encountering a block lately in my composing, a composer's block analogous to a writer's block, for the most beautiful songs are those "in which the words are like icons," the ones no one "has been able to listen to without weeping."[17] I see then it is not enough to have a method of putting words and music together, but it is necessary to be in touch with the eternal source of words and music.

What then is the source? "God's my god . . . But I find him rather too subtle . . . I don't know where he is nor what he wants."[18] Those words of Saint Thomas More in *A Man for All Seasons* state the theme of Rilke's next three stories of God, the first and second of which are Italian tales—the third Italian tale comes later. "A Scene from the Ghetto of Venice" is about an old man who climbs higher and higher with his granddaughter and her child till he can see the ocean, "Had he seen the sea or God, the eternal, in his glory?" and the children who hear the story say "Oh, the sea too."[19] And that is what it is like, trying to come into touch with the eternal source of words and music. Have we seen the sea or God, the eternal, in his glory? Oh, the sea too. As Martin Buber says, "We listen to our inmost selves—and do not know which sea we hear murmuring."[20] There I have changed the metaphor from seeing to hearing, but the question is the same, "Which sea?"

"Of One Who Listened to the Stones," the second Italian tale, is about Michelangelo listening to the stones and hearing God inside the stones. Here too the metaphor is hearing, although the metaphor of seeing is there as well, Michelangelo seeing the forms imprisoned in the stones and releasing them by his sculpture. What does he see and what does he hear? The question again. He sees the forms but he hears God. So too with the metaphor of the sea, "We listen to our inmost selves—and do not know which sea we hear murmuring." We hear the unknown, and the unknown is God. If we try to know God we are baffled, "I find him rather too subtle . . . I don't know where he is nor what he wants," but we can know the relationship with God, it seems to me, we can know "my Father and your Father," as Jesus says to Mary Magdalene, "my God and your God." And so too Saint Thomas More is able to say "God's my god." To hear God inside the stones, I think, is to know the relationship.

A third Italian tale comes later, "The Beggar and the Proud Young Lady," but at this point there is one more tale about "I don't know where he is" and that is "How the Thimble Came to Be God." A friend sent me a child's thimble from Germany in memory of this tale. According to the story, some children are playing a game in which a thimble is God and whoever has the thimble has God. In the end a little girl has the thimble but loses it and is looking for it on the ground. As evening comes she is still looking and the others have gone home. People ask her what she is looking for and she says "a thimble," but finally Someone comes and asks her and she says "I am looking for God," and that Someone takes her hand and says "And just look, what a beautiful thimble I found today."[21]

After this the tales are about where God can be found, how "There is nothing wiser than a circle" and "The God who has fled from us out of the heavens, out of the earth will he come to us again,"[22] and the first story is "A Tale of Death and a Strange Postscript Thereto," how God comes to us through death, and it ends "Now is Death flowering."[23] My vision of a great circle of life and light and love supposes too "There is nothing wiser than a circle," and though it has us moving in a circle rather than God it comes to the same thing, "Now is Death flowering." The wisdom of the circle suggests that death is an eternal return, "In my beginning is my end" and "In my end is my beginning." My vision of everything coming from God and returning to God, turned inside out, becomes the vision of Rilke, "The God who has fled from us out of the heavens, out of the earth will he come to us again."

A second story in this last group is "A Society Sprung of an Urgent Need" and seems to say God is to be found not in one alone. That seems the thought also of Martin Buber's *I and Thou*, that we each have a *thou* and *I* has its meaning in relation to *thou*, and God is the eternal *thou*. My own thinking on this is based on the Gospel of John and its formula, "I in them and thou in me," Jesus in his disciples and God in Jesus, and also on the name given in the Gospel of Matthew, Emmanuel or "God with us." So for me too, though I seem always to be speaking of one alone, God is "with us." In being "alone with the Alone," as I am in prayer, I find I am unalone. Loneliness then is my starting point, but in that loneliness there is the heart's desire to be unalone, and heart's desire is fulfilled in love coming from God and going to God.

A third story is the third Italian tale, "The Beggar and the Proud Young Lady," where God is not mentioned at all, and the implication seems to be that God is found in "the tacit dimension." "We can know more than we can tell," and that "more" is what Michael Polanyi calls "the tacit dimension." It is true, in telling all these stories of God there is always "more than we can tell." That seems implicit already in the story of the two hands, especially if I associate the right hand with words and the left hand with music. There is always more than words, and that "more" has something to do with music. It is as if words were music inside out, I have been saying, or music were words inside out, and the vision of everything coming from God and returning to God were inside out the vision of God withdrawing and coming back to us.

"A Story Told to the Dark" then is the last story of all, where "God was" and "God will be," as in the vision of God withdrawing and coming back to us. Inside out, though, this is my vision of a great circle of life and light and love, of all coming from God and all returning to God. It is "A Story Told to the Dark," for the dark holds the secret of God withdrawing and coming back to us, the secret of us coming from God and returning to God. "The love is from God and of God and towards God," the old Bedouin said to Lawrence of Arabia, and that perhaps is what Doctor Georg Lassmann is learning in this story as he seeks and finds his childhood friend Klara, their love is "from God and of God and towards God." When he asks her about the love of God, she says "Love of God?" as if this was far from her thoughts, but then she says when she came to Florence "I felt that he *was*—at some time once *was* . . ." "And now?" he asks her. "Now—now I sometimes think: He will be."[24] In childhood Georg and Klara had waited together for an important guest who never came, but now they resolve to wait together until God comes.

Loneliness is my way to God, lack and loss and letting go, lack of companionship, loss of human presences, letting go of human beings, or realizing I have to let them go, and learning to love God, to find joy in the thought of God, joy in God alone. And that, I have learned from Spinoza, is the love of God, simply joy at the thought of God, or as I feel it, joy at the thought of God being with me on my way. So all my personal memory of God is a memory of joy, remembering joy, remembering it sometimes when I have forgotten gladness and am immersed in sadness or in fear and sadness, immersed in loneliness and longing. Here are all four "perturbations of the mind,"[25] as Saint Augustine calls them, desire and gladness, fear and sadness, but love is there in the desire and the gladness.

Remembering joy, and remembering love, and that may be the same thing if love is joy at the thought of the loved one,

> Come my joy, my love, my heart,
> Such a joy as none can move,
> Such a love as none can part,
> Such a heart as joys in love.

Those lines are from one of Geoge Herbert's mystical songs, set to music by Ralph Vaughan Williams.[26] It is possible to forget joy, to forget love, to be outside your heart looking for the way back in. "Your father loves you, and will remember it ere the end," Tolkien has Gandalf say to Faramir.[27] We forget love and then remember it again; we forget joy and then remember it again; we are outside our heart and then inside it again.

Roads taken and roads not taken are there in my memory. The way of words, I have been saying, was my road taken, and the way of music my road not taken rejoining my road taken, but there were others as well. Those roads, some of them left irrevocably behind, may belong to the left hand, and I may be still in that story of the two hands, where the glove fitting the one hand will fit the other if it is turned inside out, where music belongs to "the mystery of words." I have chosen the right hand holding all truth but have also taken the left holding the lifelong pursuit of truth, and in that lifelong pursuit I find the roads I have not taken, as if to say with Tolkien, "there was only one Road, that it was like a great river: its springs were at every doorstep, and every path was its tributary."[28]

Thinking of the one Road, I can say "your hand will do all things for me," as in Psalm 138, or (in the King James Version) "The Lord will perfect that which concerneth me." Or (in the Revised Standard Version) "The Lord will fulfil his purpose for me."[29] I can rely on God to take care of all my needs, even my need for human companionship. So in all the branching paths of life I can trust God to be with me. That is my joy, that God is with me on my way, and that is my love of God, my joy at the thought of God-with-us. In choosing both hands of God, however, the right holding all truth and the left the lifelong pursuit of truth, I have gotten myself into a dialectic of "already" and "not yet," "already" in that God has spoken one Word and then kept silence, and "not yet" in that the Word is "very slowly spoken by the shining of the stars."[30]

"Even the very wise cannot see all ends,"[31] Tolkien says, meaning the ends of life, even the very wise cannot see all ends of life, see in advance how lives will turn out. Thinking then of the one road and choosing both hands of God, all truth and the lifelong pursuit, we still cannot see all ends, do not know how our lives will come out, happy ending or sad, though we can hope and pray for the happy ending. The story of God's hands, holding all truth and the lifelong pursuit, seems to say both alternatives are good and that goodness will triumph in the end over evil and lovelessness, that the happy ending, the *eucatastrophe* as Tolkien calls it, is of the essence of the story. Certainly it is of the essence of the story of God as it exists in "a Great Memory passing on from generation to generation," at least in its Christian version, for "This story begins and ends in joy."[32]

A Great Memory of God

It is true, there is a sad story of God withdrawing from us after having originally been in touch with us, and this story is a common one among many peoples. *Zimzum* (or *tsimtsum*) is the Hebrew term for this withdrawal, and the *Shekinah* is the term for the presence of God in the world, a term that also occurs in the Koran—the Arabic is similar, *Shechina*.[33] The Christian story of "God-with-us" can be seen as a story of the *Shekinah,* and the "I am" sayings of Jesus as an expression of the presence of God. "This story begins and ends in joy," beginning with the birth of the child Jesus and ending with his resurrection from the dead, and so to reject this story, as Tolkien says, "leads either to sadness or to wrath."

Sadness is there in our loneliness, lack and loss and letting go, unless we may hope, believing in the great circle of life and light and love. Wrath is there in the frustration of heart's desire apart from the great circle of its fulfilment. Everything depends then on that great circle. "I came from the Father and have come into the world; again, I am leaving the world and going to the Father," Jesus says at the Last Supper in the Gospel of John, and his disciples says "Ah, now you are speaking plainly, not in any figure!"[34] There is a story here, and "this story begins and ends in joy," for it begins and ends in God, but there is more than a story, more than a figure, there is a relationship, a relation in which we can share, "to my Father and your Father, to my God and your God." "We can know more than we can tell": we can tell this story beginning and ending in joy, but we can know the relationship, and that relationship with God leads into our own story beginning and ending in joy.

Inside out, though, as I have been saying, this story of coming from God and returning to God is the story of God withdrawing from us and coming back again to us, and there are traces of that story too in the story of Jesus, as when he exclaims in the words of the psalm, "My God, my God, why hast thou forsaken me?"[35] We too can feel the traces of that story, "A Story Told to the Dark," we can feel the sadness, the frustration of heart's desire, we can say, like Georg and Klara in Rilke's story, "God was" and "God will be," and we can resolve to wait together until God comes. "I'm thinking that it's like that evening once more," Georg says: "*you are again waiting for the wonderful guest, for God, and know that he will come—* And I have joined you by chance—" and Klara says "Well, this time we'll really wait until it happens."[36]

Waiting on God is living in the great circle of life and light and love. "Waiting for Godot," on the other hand, as in Samuel Beckett's play, is a waiting that is dominated by the sadness and the frustration—Godot never comes. "Let's go / We can't / Why not? / We're waiting for Godot"[37] Is there an essential difference here? I want to say there is, in the relationship with God primarily and then in the story itself. Are we waiting for something to happen, some outward occurrence that will change our lives and make us new persons, or are we waiting for an illumining of mind and a kindling of heart?

"All life weighed in the scales of my own life," Yeats concluded in an autobiography, "seems to me a preparation for something that never happens."[38] That was before the experience he relates in *A Vision.* "I came to believe in a Great Memory passing on from generation to generation," he says, and that was the preparation for *A Vision*. My own vision of a great circle of life and light and love comes too of opening my mind to "a Great Memory passing on from generation to generation," counting the Gospels and particularly the Gospel of John as "a Great Memory." I realize that much is made nowadays of the Gnostic Gospels which have been found but have not been "passing on from generation to generation" as tradition. To me, though, it seems important that the canonical Gospels have been passing through many minds over the ages. This is a kind of testing and verification of their truth.

"Test everything; hold fast what is good"[39]—I found those words underlined in a family Bible. The words of the Gospel have been tested and found good and held fast, and in particular "the words of eternal life," and they have indeed become "a Great Memory passing on from generation to generation." The testing is a matter of living in the relationship of Jesus with his God Abba, dwelling in the particulars of that relation, the name, the kingdom, the will, the bread, the forgiveness, the guiding and guarding from temptation and evil. If I am dwelling in those particulars, I am testing it and finding it good and holding it fast. I am "proving the unseen"[40] as George MacDonald says, as in the King James version of those words, "Prove all things; hold fast that which is good."

Waiting on God then is dwelling in the particulars of the great circle of life and light and love. Waiting for Godot, on the other hand, is waiting for something to happen, maybe (as in this time of terror) for something dreadful to occur, or then again maybe waiting simply for a call or a letter or a meeting. What waiting for Godot prevents you from doing, as in that brief dialogue ("Let's go / We can't / Why not? / We're waiting for Godot"), is going on. It is said the last words of the Buddha to his disciples were "Walk on!"[41] Waiting on God too is a way of going on, walking on with God in life and light and love, waiting only on the kindling of the heart and the illumining of the mind, letting God take the lead. What then of the dreadful? Perhaps we can say we live in a world where the dreadful has already occurred. We wait then not on the dreadful but on the light, on the sunrise of life and light and love.

If everything that happened were the will of God, as in the common notion of God, then the story of God would be simply the story of what happens. If things can happen against the will of God, on the other hand, if God is vulnerable, then the story of God is quite a different one, a story of the illumining of minds and the kindling of hearts, of rekindling hearts in a world that grows chill through sin and lovelessness. The story of God then is that of a great circle of life and light and love. Yet how is this circle related to what happens? It passes through what happens, I suppose, in that God can draw good out of evil, for instance can draw a spiritual renewal out of an outbreak of terrorism.

"Human history becomes more and more a race between education and catastrophe,"[42] H. G. Wells said at the end of his *Outline of History.* Education, Yes, and not just the illumining of minds but also the kindling and rekindling of hearts. Catastrophe, Yes, "a world that grows chill," and catastrophic destruction. If *Stories of God* are a personal memory, Rilke's *Duino Elegies* are his sense of a Great Memory, though the central figure is not God but the angel. This contrast is also present in ancient stories, Will God go with his people or will he send an angel (Exodus 33)? At any rate, the angel too is a formidable figure. For me, nevertheless, the hope has always been that God is with me, that my life is a journey in time and God is my companion on the way, "God-with-us," and if not, "Who, if I cried out, would hear me among the angelic orders?"[43] as Rilke begins his elegies.

"Angels," he goes on to say, "often don't know whether they move among the living or the dead."[44] That is because the souls of the dead are alive, and that goes with the idea of God as God of the living to whom all are alive. Human beings, though, as he goes on to say in the Second Elegy, human beings in love and in death, as he reflects on unrequited love and early death, do not have the kind of hold on being that angels have. "To have and to hold" is just what we can never seem to do, but human life is all about letting go and letting be, or as he says later in the Eighth Elegy, "we live our lives forever taking leave."[45] That is certainly my own experience. My life is a journey in time, and God is my companion on the way, but I seem indeed to live my life forever taking leave. There is a sadness in taking leave, but there is a gladness in the thought of God being with me on the way. That is the essence of the love of God, as I have been learning from Spinoza, joy at the thought of God.

Dark forces within us are the theme of the Third Elegy, dark forces at work in love and in death. These forces are present too in ancient stories of human beings coming to know good and evil and God withdrawing from us. God's withdrawal goes with the unleashing of these dark forces. His presence was like the presence of the mother in Rilke's elegy, soothing the child and calming all its fears. His absence allows us to feel at once the fear and the fascination of the dark forces in love and death. Dread and fascination are the dark forces of attraction and repulsion, and that is the definition of the Holy according to Rudolf Otto, *mysterium tremendum et fascinandum,* but it goes with God's withdrawal, for the mystery "shows itself and at the same time withdraws."[46] No doubt, terrorism is the use of these dark forces to gain power, and as Tolkien says of the Black Riders, "their power is in terror."[47]

My own experience of withdrawal is of human presences in my life being withdrawn, while God is always there for me, and so I don't want to speak like Jung of a dark side of God but of a dark side of human relations. That is the theme of the Fourth Elegy, a dark side of human relations, a puppet show and watching a puppet show. I think however of Kleist's essay "On the Marionette Theatre." All love, I want to say, is encompassed in the love of God *on the path taken by the soul of the dancer,*[48] as Kleist calls it there, imagining marionettes with only one string attached to their center of gravity so when they are drawn along a straight path their limbs describe circles. It is true, this is turning the puppet show into a positive image of grace and human relations into the love of God. The dark side gets absorbed in the dance.

But can the dark side of human relations be absorbed in the dance? "Saltimbanques," the Fifth Elegy, explores what happens "on the path taken by the soul of the dancer." It is based on Picasso's painting and on Rilke's memory of a troop of acrobats. My own experience is of composing song and dance cycles and of performing them with singers and dancers and me on the piano, not dancing myself but participating in the exaltation of the dance, I suppose somewhat like Rilke looking at Picasso's painting and watching the acrobats. I see it as learning to love "with all your might," like David who "danced before the Lord with all his might." The dark side of human relations comes up especially in learning to love "with all your soul," learning detachment in love, but then you go on learning to love "with all your might" and that seems to bring wholeness in love.

> O body swayed to music, O brightening glance,
> How can we know the dancer from the dance?

I found myself playing on these words of Yeats in four dances with words I wrote for a song cycle called *The King of the Golden River:*

Dance of the Winds
O guiding eye,
O guarding storm,
how can we know
the spirit from the wind?

Fire Dance
O lonely wish,
impassioned hope,
how can we know
the spirit from the flame?

Earth Dance
O mystery
that shows and then withdraws,
how can we know
the spirit from the dance?

River Dance
O spring of water
welling up into eternal life,
how can we know
the spirit from the thirst?[49]

Yes, so there is wholeness in the dance, but that is in the moment of the dance. What about otherwise? I know my dancers, how they too have lives apart from dance. In the Sixth Elegy Rilke is looking for lives where the dancer does not exist apart from the dance, the life of the hero, the death of the youthful dead. To love God, though, is to have a relationship with God, and that relationship is abiding, even when I am not actually dancing with all my might.

What then of the dark forces apart from the dance? I know, the real dark forces are dread and fascination, when they are used to gain power, but I was thinking especially of the withdrawal of human presences in my life, and I begin to understand how this reflects "the road not taken" in my life and my own choice of the road taken. Taking responsibility for my own life, I can see this dark side of my relations with others as my own shadow. As Rilke begins in his Seventh Elegy, "No longer let wooing send forth your cry: you're past that."[50] I have to realize that I have made the choice of the road taken, and this choice has consequences. It is true, I can hope the road taken will rejoin the road not taken, as my way of words has rejoined my way of music, for instance in the very dances mentioned above. Maybe it is in those moments of dance when we cannot know the dancer from the dance that the roads rejoin. I have to let go, though, of "wooing," of playing with the road not taken as if I were going to take it.

"We live our lives forever taking leave," Rilke's conclusion in the Eighth Elegy, is true of things passing in our lives and also of the letting go of the road not taken which seems never to be finally left behind. It is as if I had to choose ever and again the road taken and let go again and again of the road not taken. The rejoining of the roads, nevertheless, my experience of the way of words rejoining the way of music, seems to belong to the idea "there was only one Road; that it was like a great river: its springs were at every doorstep, and every path was its tributary." We live our lives then forever taking leave, for "the road goes ever on and on." There is a letting go that is a letting be, and there is an openness to the mystery, to the unknown ahead, and the openness embodies a hope that is open to the unhoped-for, as in the saying of Heraclitus, "Unless you hope, you will not find the unhoped-for."[51]

We are turned around, Rilke says, "looking at, never out of, everything."[52] It is in facing the Open, as he calls it, that we find the unhoped-for, but we are always turned around, facing the world, facing the future, facing death. That is why "we live our lives forever taking leave," looking back, like Lot's wife looking back at Sodom and being turned into a pillar of salt. I suppose looking back means living in time and that includes looking forward, facing the future and facing death, whereas looking into the Open seems to mean living in the present or living in the Presence or living in the Presence in the present. I guess that is what is meant too in the Gospels by not looking back and taking no thought for the morrow. What comes of this? The earth, Rilke says in the Ninth Elegy, arises invisibly in us. We turn matter into spirit.

To turn matter into spirit, he seems to be saying in the Tenth and last Elegy, is to turn sorrow into joy, to go through sorrow to joy. An elegy was a song of mourning or lamentation in ancient times accompanied by a flute, and so in this last elegy Rilke is speaking of elegy itself, how the matter of our sorrow is transformed into spirit and joy by being expressed in poetry, as "emotion recollected in tranquillity." My own joy, I find, is the love of God, joy at the thought of God, joy at being with God on the way, and my own sadness, my sense of lack and loss and letting go, is absorbed in the joy of being on the journey with God. I don't seem quite to share Rilke's intense feeling for unrequited love and youthful death, but my sadness seems to be essentially that of loneliness. The longing in my loneliness, though, becomes love, the love of God, and so turns into joy, and that is how I turn matter into spirit, going from sadness to gladness through my vision of a journey with God in time.

"Do you still remember God?" Rilke's question in his *Stories of God* points to a personal memory, therefore, and also to "a Great memory passing on from generation to generation," but there is also another meaning of "remembering God," *dikhr Allah* in Islam, which means calling God to mind or keeping God in mind, like the people I met in Istanbul telling their prayer beads. For me keeping

God in mind is keeping in mind God-with-us, keeping in mind my journey with God in time. It is remembering joy, the joy of being with God on the way. It becomes essential in times of sadness and of fear and of unfulfilled desire to remember gladness, to recover joy. So for me it becomes more and more imperative, as my life goes on and the things of life are passing from my life, to live in the standpoint of the person before God rather than in that of the person before others or even that of the person before self. It is like the practice in Islam of meditating on the ninety-nine names of God, but I meditate really on the one name of God-with-us.

Divine names are a memory theatre, the ninety-nine in Islam, the ten in the Kabbalah. I remember once going at night with two young Jewish women to meet a Sufi master on the Mount of Olives. When we approached, he was sitting and meditating in front of a large picture with the ninety-nine names of God inscribed upon it. He turned to us and said "You can ask," and his advice to us in the end was "Go deep in your own religion." I took it that I was to go deep in Christianity and the two young women were to go deep in Judaism and the Sufi master himself was to go deep in Islam, and that we would all meet in God. Remembering God, I take it, is going deep, for it leads you into the realm of spirit.

"God is spirit"

Take this ring, Master, for your labours will be heavy; but it will
support you in the weariness that you have taken upon yourself.
For this is the Ring of Fire, and with it you may rekindle hearts
in a world that grows chill.

—J. R. R. Tolkien

◆ "God is spirit,"[1] Jesus tells the woman at the well, and God
acts spiritually, I want to conclude, illumining minds and kindling
hearts. This is a very different conception of God, I gather, from
the ordinary one that everything that happens is the will of God.
According to this we live "in a world that grows chill" through sin
and lovelessness, and God works against this, illumining minds
and kindling hearts, and we can work with God, as Cirdan tells
Gandalf, "you may rekindle hearts in a world that grows chill."[2]

What of creation and God as creator? Creation is a relationship, I want to say, and spirit is relatedness. And what of divine
providence? That too is a matter of relatedness. What I mean is
that everything is related to God and God is related to everything
and so God does not have to intervene from the outside in order to
act but acts through that relatedness that is already there, as in the
prayer

God be in my head, and in my understanding;
God be in my eyes, and in my looking;

God be in my mouth, and in my speaking;
God be in my heart, and in my thinking;
God be at my end, and at my departing.[3]

The prayer is not "God is in . . ." but "God be in . . ." as if God has to be asked into our lives. So too in the prayer "Thy will be done on earth as it is in heaven," as if it were not necessarily done on earth unless we do it. So not everything that happens is the will of God, as if everything were in accord with the relationship with God. On the contrary, things happen against the will of God, terrible things, and so *God is vulnerable,* as I heard Jacques Maritain once say. God is vulnerable by choice, I mean, creating us free and creating our world and giving it and us real existence.

If we explore the idea of spirit more in depth, as Hegel does in his *Phenomenology of Spirit,* "pure self-recognition in absolute otherness,"[4] the human counterpart of "God is spirit," we find human relatedness to reside in the "I and thou," as Martin Buber says, so that "I" depends on "thou" for its meaning. God is "the eternal thou," as Buber says, and so gives final meaning to "I am," or to stay with the Gospel of John the meaning of "God is spirit" is spelled out in the formula at the Last Supper, "I in them and thou in me," where "I" is Jesus and "thou" is Abba, his God, and "them" are the disciples. Spirit is relatedness, but in Christianity the relationship for us is ultimately one of us entering into that of Jesus with his God. That relationship is for us the full realization of everything related to God and God to everything.

God acts spiritually then, I want to say, illumining minds and kindling hearts and rekindling hearts "in a world that grows chill." There is a hint of this in the creation story in Genesis where God's first words in the Bible are "Let there be light." This is how God is in my understanding and my looking and my speaking and my thinking and at my departing, as in the prayer from the Sarum Missal. Is it enough to say this is how God is present among us? I think of the words of the High One in a story by Patricia McKillip, "Beyond logic, beyond reason, beyond hope. Trust me."[5]

Illumining Minds

God be in my hede:
and in myn understandynge.

"I know. But . . . I don't understand," Avremel says in *The Trial of God* by Elie Wiesel. "All your life you tried to entertain. To make people laugh," Mendel answers. "To do so you had to learn to know them—not to understand them."[6] To go from knowing to understanding is an illumining of the mind. To ask God "to be in my head, and in my understanding" is to ask for that illumining. There are times when I can say too "I know. But . . . I don't understand," especially when others withdraw from my life. I know them but I don't understand them. God is in this too insofar as I pray and ask God to help, but God's reply seems usually to be "I am with you." What then is the understanding? I suppose it is an understanding of my own life as much as of others, of my own journey with God in time.

Passing over has been my way of coming to understand others, entering into the standpoint of the other, passing over into lives and times, into cultures, into religions, and then coming back with new insight to my own standpoint. Why then am I baffled by others withdrawing from my life? I guess it is because I have not passed over but wrongly assumed with persons near to me that their standpoint was the same as my own, whereas in the encounter with other cultures and other religions and in the study of literary figures I realize the distance and that I have to pass over. If then I do try to pass over to those near, I find it is not so easy to separate them from my own life. Self-knowledge is indeed the key to understanding, to know where I end and where they begin. It is said of King Lear "he hath ever but slenderly known himself."[7]

"I know who I am," Don Quixote says, coming back from his first sally. Then "I have been enchanted," he says, coming back from his second sally. And then finally "I was mad, and now I'm sane," he says, returning from his third and last sally and lying on his deathbed. Jacques Lacan calls this final state of having lost all one's illusions "subjective destitution."[8] Actually, though, Don Quixote still has his faith on his deathbed and he dies at peace with God, not at all what Lacan had in mind. For me too, self-knowledge is not simply a state of disillusionment in the standpoint of the person before self but is essentially the insight that comes in the standpoint of the person before God, like the self-knowledge of Saint Augustine in his *Confessions*. Saint Augustine's prayer in his *Soliloquies*, "May I know me! May I know thee!" is answered in his *Confessions* in and by the standpoint of the person before God.

So when I ask God to be in my understanding, I am asking for the illumination of mind that comes in the standpoint of the person before God. What then of my bafflement at persons withdrawing from my life? In the standpoint before God I see my life as a journey with God in time. I see the things of my life entering and passing from my life, persons too entering and passing, but the journey goes ever on and on, as Tolkien says, "the Road goes ever on and on." So when someone withdraws from my life, it does not have the significance it would have in the standpoint of the person before others, an essential loss, or in that of the person before self, that I am still there myself, but I seem to be learning detachment in love, letting be and openness to the mystery that "shows itself and at the same time withdraws." It is like letting go of everyone and everything on the deathbed, like Don Quixote at the end.

> God be in myn eyen:
> and in my lokynge.

"More light!" Goethe's last words seem significant here, and the idea of "catching the light,"[9] that we don't see light itself but we see things in the light. For light is one of the three great metaphors in the Gospel of John, life and light and love, and Saint Augustine's theory of illumination, as I understand it, is that we see things in the perpetual light of God when we know them. It is not that we have already in this life the blessed vision of God, a common misinterpretation of the theory, especially by those who reject it. We do not see God's light itself but we see things in God's light. It is like physical light traveling through outer space—we see only darkness unless an object is interposed and illuminated. So it is with spiritual light, we see things *in* the perpetual light.

I use the term "perpetual light" from the funeral liturgy, *Requiem dona eis, Domine: et lux perpetua luceat eis,* "Eternal rest give them O Lord, and let perpetual light shine upon them." I think too of the work of Franz Cumont, who wrote *After Life in Roman Paganism* and then in later life became a believer and wrote a new edition of the book with the title *Lux Perpetua*.[10] "After Life" was the term in his skeptical years and "Perpetual Light" was the term when he came to believe in eternal life. If Saint Augustine is on the right track, that we know things in the perpetual light, then we have an actual experience of the perpetual light in our knowing, though we don't see the light by itself but see things in the light. So it is not easy to discern the light itself, though we are seeing things in the light, and even less easy to discern that the light is perpetual.

"Attention," as Malebranche has said, "is the natural prayer of the soul,"[11] and attention, we could say, is our way of discerning the divine light. By attending to the light in which we see what we know, we attend to God and knowing becomes prayer, and we know in the standpoint of the person before God. It is possible also to know in the standpoint before self and even in that before others. It is in the standpoint before God, though, that we become conscious of the divine light, and this is where Saint Augustine seems to have come to his theory of illumination, writing his *Confessions,* where he is using the language of the Psalms and in particular the language of Psalm 4 about being signed with the light of the divine countenance. He met some kind of writer's block in his earlier works and most of them were left unfinished, but in his *Confessions* he seems to have found his voice and it is that of a person before God.

So when I ask God to be in my eyes and in my looking, I am asking to see or to look upon everyone and everything from the standpoint before God. Saint Augustine speaks of the divine light and of the blind Tobit and the blind Isaac and the blind Jacob seeing and sets that over and against "the lust of the eyes" and "looking upon with lust" in his *Confessions*.[12] For myself I have connected "a wandering eye" in my life with "a divided heart" and "a stifled cry"—those are the terms I have used—and I suppose the answer to all three is to live in the standpoint before God.

> God be in my mouth:
> and in my spekynge.

"A stifled cry" is the cry of the heart. "Within our whole universe the story only has authority to answer that cry of heart of its characters," as Isak Dinesen says, "that one cry of heart of each of them: *Who am I?*"[13] It is by telling my story that I utter my stifled cry. Is that really my cry of heart, though, *Who am I?* If loneliness is being alone and longing to be unalone, and to be unalone is to be understood, and being myself I do not fully understand myself and long to be understood by another, then my cry of heart is indeed *Who am I?* It is a cry to be unalone, to be understood. So then telling my story is my way of coming to understand and to be understood. "We can know more than we can tell," though, as I keep quoting from Polanyi, and that seems to point beyond the story to the relationship and to the relationship with God, but there mystery in the true sense gets into who I am. So the cry of heart becomes Saint Augustine's prayer, "May I know me! May I know thee!"

An answer to the prayer is to tell my story, as Saint Augustine tells his, from the standpoint before God, to cast the story into the form of prayer. Or more simply, prayer is an answer, to turn my ongoing lonely conversation with myself into a conversation with God. A friend of mine says prayer is listening to God tell our story—this gets close to the monastic life with its combination of praying the Psalms and "divine reading" (*lectio divina*), the Psalms us speaking to God and "divine reading" God speaking to us, where it is true as in all reading "we read to know that we are not alone." Perhaps the answer to our loneliness is, like Plato's philosophy, "an endless conversation."[14] There is the conversation with others and there is the conversation with ourselves and there is the conversation with God. Every one of them is some kind of answer to loneliness, but the conversation with God is an answer to the deep loneliness that is not taken away even in human intimacy.

"An endless conversation" is an *I and thou*, certainly what Martin Buber had in mind by *I and thou*, and if reading too is a conversation and "divine reading" a conversation with God, it may be the place where the prayer to know me and to know thee is answered. Saint Augustine put the prayer in his *Soliloquies* in a conversation with himself but found the answer in his *Confessions* in a conversation with God. It is true, he did the talking there and yet the other element is there too, God speaking, in his reading, responding to the command "Take and read!"[15] What I understand by "divine reading," *lectio divina,* as practiced in the monastic life, is reading the scriptures and letting them speak to the heart. It can include other reading too, if you let it speak to the heart.

So when I ask God to be in my mouth and in my speaking, I am asking to be able to speak from the standpoint before God, to be able to pray. I have often wondered why Saint Augustine does not continue to speak and write from this standpoint after his *Confessions,* for he showed there not only how you can tell your own story but also how you can reflect on time and memory and Genesis from that standpoint. Yet he does not cast his later works into the form of prayer but simply into the form of essay. I find it difficult myself to speak and write in the form of prayer unless I am casting what I say into verse. "Tell us your tale," Elrond says to Bilbo. "And if you have not yet cast your story into verse, you may tell it in plain words."[16]

God be in my herte:
and in my thynkynge.

"Thinking is thanking," the mystic saying of the seventeenth century that Heidegger is always quoting, suggests that thinking too can be from the standpoint before God. That may be the answer to "a divided heart." "Noble-mindedness would be the nature of thinking and thereby of thanking," the Scholar says in "A Conversation on a Country Path," and Heidegger answers "Of that thinking which does not have to thank for something, but only thanks for being allowed to thank."[17] My own understanding of "Thinking is thanking" is thanking for something or really for everyone and everything in my life, as in Dag Hammarskjöld's "For all that has been—Thanks!" It is thinking, as in the saying "Count your blessings!" Thus "Thinking is thanking" for me means recollecting your life with thanks, and the thanks is a way of relating to the past, "For all that has been." What Heidegger has in mind is recollection too, "thinking back," but thinking back to Being, not *how* things are but *that* they are, and so it is thanking that they are.

"A divided heart" is a heart torn by regret and fear, regret of the past and fear of the future, and so "For all that has been— Thanks! To all that shall be—Yes!" is a direct answer, as Tolkien says, "To cast aside regret and fear."[18] Regret is of the road not taken. So thanking for the road taken is casting aside regret. Thanking that "thanks only for being allowed to thank" is thanking that things *are* rather than for how they are, and so it too leaves behind regret and fear which are about *how* things are. It is, so to speak, an indirect answer to regret and fear by directing our thinking to a different point of origin, to Being rather than to beings.

Thinking back to Being for me is thinking back to the wonder of existence I experienced in childhood when I lay looking up at the stars on summer nights. There was the wonder of the world's existence and the wonder of my own existence, it is and I am. This thinking becomes thanking for existence, a thanking that "thanks only for being allowed to thank," and it is a casting aside of regret and fear. "There, peeping among the cloud-wrack above a dark tor high up in the mountains, Sam saw a white star twinkle for a while," Tolkien tells. "The beauty of it smote his heart, as he looked up out of the forsaken land, and hope returned to him. For like a shaft, clear and cold, the thought pierced him that in the end the Shadow was only a small and passing thing: there was light and high beauty for ever beyond its reach."[19] It was a casting aside especially of fear. "Now, for a moment, his own fate, and even his master's, ceased to trouble him."

So when I ask God to be in my heart and in my thinking, I am asking to live in the wonder of existence, to live without regret and fear. Is that the same as living in the standpoint before God? Not for Heidegger, but it is for me. I think of Wittgenstein's saying, "Not *how* the world is, is the mystical, but *that* it is" and "The feeling of the world as a limited whole is the mystical feeling" and "There is indeed the inexpressible. This *shows* itself; it is the mystical."[20] To live in the wonder of existence is to live in the feeling of the mystical and that is to live in the standpoint before God. But is it possible to live without regret and fear? To do so, I have to deal also with *how* the world is or *how* things are, I have to relate to the past and to the future, "For all that has been—Thanks! To all that shall be—Yes!" And even at that I can still feel regret and fear, but "the mystical feeling" is stronger, and in that sense "love casts out fear" and "love is letting go of fear."

> God be at myn ende:
> and at my departynge.

What fear? The fear that comes "at my end and at my departing." The casting out or the letting go of fear is as in those words "Now, for a moment, his own fate, and even his master's, ceased to trouble him." It is the fear surrounding one's fate. "What is it to have one's own death in each case?" Heidegger asks. "It is Dasein's running ahead to its past," he answers, "to an extreme possibility of itself that stands before it in certainty and utter indeterminacy" and "This running ahead is nothing other than the authentic and singular future of one's own Dasein."[21] Dasein, "being there," is his name for human existence. So he reflects on my end and my departing, not on God being there but on me "being there" at my own end and my own departing, and so from the standpoint before myself and not before God.

If then I ask God to be there at my end and at my departing, I am shifting to the standpoint before God. Do the things Heidegger says about "being there" still hold before God? He speaks of being in the world, everydayness, disposition, care, authenticity, death, uncanniness, temporality, and historicity. After starting with the question "What is time?" he comes in conclusion to the question "Are we ourselves time?" and "Am I my time?" and he wants to answer "Yes."[22] In the standpoint before God, however, we come rather to a sense of eternal life, a sense that "eternal life belongs to those who live in the present," as Wittgenstein says, or rather, as I have been saying, "eternal life belongs to those who live in the presence." And if I see the standpoint before God, as I have been doing, as an entering into the relation of Jesus with his God, the God of the living to whom the dead are alive, as he argues with the Sadducees, I see I am not my time, which comes to an end "at my end," but I am *in* my time, and what happens "at my departing" is an eternal return, a going home to God.

"Being there," as Heidegger describes it, is "being-in-the-world." I think of Jerzy Kosinski's novel *Being There* and the comedy film based on it with Peter Sellers about a man who has known nothing but watching television and tending a garden, and his patron dies and he has to go out into the world.[23] So the novel and the film are about being there in the world. All the things Heidegger says about "being there," everydayness, disposition, care, authenticity, death, uncanniness, temporality, and historicity, are predicated on being there in the world. Eternal life, on the other hand, and an eternal return, a going home to God would simply carry us beyond the world if it were not for the possibility of living in the standpoint before God already in this life, as Saint Augustine is doing in his *Confessions,* the possibility of *living in the presence in the present.* So too eternal life, as it is conceived in the

Gospel of John, begins already in this life and before death, and points on to an eternal return, a going home to God in death.

So when I ask God to be there with me at my end and at my departing, I am asking for an eternal return, for going home to God in death. "In sorrow we must go, but not in despair," Tolkien has Aragorn say as he lay dying. "Behold! we are not bound for ever to the circles of the world, and beyond them is more than memory. Farewell!"[24] I suppose the very fact that we are conscious of "being there" and can speak of "being-in-the-world" shows that "we are not bound for ever to the circles of the world." The satire on "being there" by Kosinski and Sellers helps too in getting beyond the seriousness of Heidegger's "being there." Of course it is even easier to satirize Tolkien's epic style and to satirize images of heaven. Still, there is hope in saying "we are not bound for ever to the circles of the world, and beyond them is more than memory."

Kindling Hearts

| Nada te turbe, | Nothing disturb you, |
| Nada te espante | Nothing affright you |

Hope and fear carry us into the realm of the heart. Saint Teresa's prayer or her meditation—it is as if God were speaking—"Nothing disturb you, Nothing affright you . . ."[25] calls for a casting out of fear or a letting go of fear. Kierkegaard, on the other hand, speaks of "dread as a saving experience by means of faith"[26] and that seems to be behind Heidegger's more secular concept of dread as an essential element of "being there." What Kierkegaard has in mind is what he calls "possibility" and that too is Heidegger's view. Dread or fear is the experience of possibility. Hope too, we could say, is an experience of possibility. "Dasein as human life is primarily being possible," Heidegger says, and death is "the indeterminate certainty of its ownmost possibility of being at an end."[27] And so dread is primarily fear of death, he thinks, but hope too, we could say, is primarily hope of eternal life. Our destiny is death/ eternal life, and concern about our fate is concern about death/ eternal life.

Dread as "a saving experience by means of faith" is a V experience, a going down and a coming up. "He sank absolutely," Kierkegaard says of "the pupil of possibility," "but then in turn he floated up from the depth of the abyss, lighter now than all that is oppressive and dreadful in life."[28] This V experience with dread and with possibility is thus a kindling of the heart, and it is this kindling of the heart that enables us to cast out fear or to let go of fear. It is a going down into dread and a coming up out of dread that leaves dread behind and one is "lighter now than all that is oppressive and dreadful in life." It is like Dante's experience of going down in *Inferno,* coming up in *Purgatorio,* where he becomes lighter and lighter as his heart is purified, until he is finally flying in *Paradiso.* "In his eyes there was peace now," Tolkien says of Frodo after he has gotten rid of the Ring, "neither strain of will, nor madness, nor any fear. His burden was taken away."[29]

It is "by means of faith" that dread becomes "a saving experience," and so without faith there is no V experience of going down and coming up but simply a living with dread. If I am *in* my time, I can go down and come up, but if I *am* my time, I carry it with me wherever I go and the dread that goes with time goes with me. "The philosopher does not believe," Heidegger says, and "if the philosopher asks about time, then he has resolved to understand time in terms of time"[30] and not in terms of eternity. It is only if I can live in the standpoint before God, only if I can live in the eternity, the timelessness, of existing before God, that I can go down and come up like Dante in *The Divine Comedy* and can come thus to the love that moves the world, the love that casts out fear or that lets go of fear, and even then I can still feel fear. It is just that the love is greater than fear.

If the love of God is simply joy at the thought of God, as Spinoza says, then it is joy that displaces fear, that casts aside regret and fear—joy, I would say, at the thought of being on a journey with God in time. So time is still there in the standpoint before God, time as "a changing image of eternity" or God in time, eternity in time, and Saint Augustine can talk about time in his *Confessions,* speaking from the standpoint before God and that before self. When Saint Teresa says "Nothing disturb you, Nothing affright you" she is speaking from that standpoint before God, or letting God speak, and she goes on to say

Todo se pasa,	All is passing,
Dios no se muda,	God unchanging,

"Only connect!"[31] E. M. Forster says, but everything depends on what you connect with, the passing or the unchanging. "The world of the happy is quite another than that of the unhappy,"[32] Wittgenstein says, for the happy connect with the unchanging, I think, but the unhappy connect with the passing. Or that is my experience: when I rely on human relations I become unhappy because of lack and loss and letting go, lack of companionship, loss of others who have been present in my life, and letting go or having to let go or get rid of what I haven't got, but when I rely on God I become happy with the joy that Spinoza speaks of, joy at the simple thought of God, for me joy at the thought of God being my companion on the way, God being there for me. Forster's idea of connecting, though, is more like relying on human relations:

Only connect! That was the whole of her sermon. Only connect the prose and the passion, and both will be exalted, and human love will be seen at its height. Live in fragments no longer. Only connect, and the beast and the monk, robbed of the isolation that is life to either, will die.

"Only connect the prose and the passion," the thinking and the feeling, that is, "and both will be exalted," for that is the meaning of "heart," not simply feeling but thinking and feeling united when they are both respected and come together, "and human love

will be seen at its height," the height not of pure feeling but of a
thinking heart. I agree with all that, "Live in fragments no longer,"
but when he goes on to say "Only connect, and the beast and the
monk, robbed of the isolation that is life to either, will die," I want
to say "Not so fast!" Yes, connect, for spirit is relatedness, but God
is spirit, and the height of love is the love of God where you love
"with all your heart, and with all your soul, and with all your
might." Instead of "the beast and the monk," you could say "flesh
and spirit," and I want both to live and to come together in a thinking heart.

   "I cannot stop searching for the great redeeming formula. For
the one word that sums up everything within me, the overflowing
and rich sense of life," Etty Hillesum writes in her diary, "... *the
thinking heart of the barracks.*"³³ Here is where I got that phrase
"a thinking heart," and I want to say it describes a union of flesh
and spirit, a union of feeling and thinking. In Etty's use of the
phrase, "the thinking heart of the barracks," it means a light shining in the darkness of the concentration camp. But apart from that
context it is a "word that sums up everything," that describes an
"overflowing and rich sense of life" simply because it means a
union of feeling and thinking. How? "All violent feelings have the
same effect. They produce in us a falseness in all our impressions
of external things," Ruskin says, "which I would generally charac-
terize as the 'pathetic fallacy'."³⁴ The union of feeling and thinking
thus takes place in the opposite, an inner peace of mind and heart
and soul.

   A thinking heart, then, knows "All is passing, God unchanging" and connects with the unchanging, though it connects also
with the passing, and so embraces both the joy and the sorrow of
life. There is then a combination of letting be and openness to mystery, as Heidegger says in his later work on thinking, where he says
also "Thinking is thanking," but I want to take that term "letting
be" (*Gelassenheit*) that he derived from Meister Eckhart rather in
its full religious meaning as Eckhart used it to mean a "Thanks!"
and a "Yes!" to God and so to connect the passing with the un-

changing. "All is passing, God unchanging" therefore, but the response of a thinking heart is "Thanks!" and "Yes!" and there is hope
in this, for

La paciencia   Patience
Todo lo alcanza.   Attains to all.

"All the unhappiness of humans comes from one thing," Pascal
says, "not knowing how to remain quietly in a room."³⁵ Happiness
then comes of the opposite, knowing how to remain quietly in
a room. To do so I have to know how to connect with the unchanging while connecting also with the passing. "You do not need to
leave your room. Remain sitting at your table and listen. Do not
even listen, simply wait. Do not even wait, be quite still and solitary," Kafka says. "The world will freely offer itself to you to be
unmasked, it has no choice, it will roll in ecstasy at your feet."³⁶ Remain quietly in a room, Kafka is saying , but to do so I have to *know
how* to remain quietly in a room, as Pascal says, I have to know
how to connect. That is the meaning, I think, of "Patience attains
to all."

To connect with the unchanging while connecting also with
the passing I have to be in the standpoint before God. It is possible
to remain quietly in a room in the standpoint before self but there
I connect only with the passing. In the standpoint before God I
connect not only with God but also with all else, with the passing
as well as the unchanging, as in the Psalms, where all human concerns are brought before God. There is peace in remaining quietly
in a room, "emotion recollected in tranquillity," and in that peace,
"in tranquillity," feeling and thinking are united, "emotion" is "recollected." Knowing how to remain quietly in a room is knowing
how to recollect emotion in tranquillity. Goethe's method of turning the truth of a life into poetry thus is a way of remaining quietly
in a room, but Saint Augustine's method of turning the truth of a
life into prayer is a way of connecting with the unchanging as well
as with the passing.

If I follow Goethe's method of turning the truth of my life into poetry, I do connect with the passing in my life. "My peace is gone, my heart is heavy,"[37] Goethe has Gretchen say in famous lines from *Faust,* and formulates there something of the experience of the passing. The emotion recollected in tranquillity is still the emotion of lost peace and a heavy heart, and yet it is recollected in tranquillity, and so there is a going beyond the unhappiness of the lost peace and the heavy heart to a peace and a tranquil heart without, for all that, connecting with the unchanging or coming before God. So this is a method of remaining quietly in a room and coming to a happiness without resorting to prayer and to faith.

If I follow Saint Augustine's method of turning the truth of my life into prayer, that too can mean turning truth into poetry. I found it easier to write in verse from the standpoint before God than to write in prose, or it can be a kind of prose poem like the *Confessions* or it can be in music like Stravinsky's *Symphony of Psalms.* Or it can be simply in prayer not written but spoken, not spoken but silent. I can see a difference, nevertheless, between recollecting your life before God, on the one hand, and becoming absorbed in God, on the other, and forgetting all else. I think of "the cloud of forgetting" in *The Cloud of Unknowing* and of the Sufis I saw dancing once in a little mosque in Jerusalem, chanting Allah! Allah! and it seemed to me forgetting all else. There are two different methods here, one of remembering your life in the presence of God, the other of remembering God and forgetting all else. In both "Patience attains to all," and

Quien a Dios tiene   One who holds to God
      Nada le falta.   Lacks nothing.

Or it could be translated, "One who *has* God lacks nothing." I think of Tolstoy writing in his diary "God is my desire."[38] It is quite something ro come to realize God is my heart's desire, for it seems many other things are what I desire. "It is amazing," Tolstoy says in "The Kreutzer Sonata," "how complete is the delusion that beauty is goodness."[39] To realize God is what my heart desires I have to break through that delusion and others. It is a step toward realization to know "All is passing, God unchanging," to know the beauty that fascinates me is passing. The trouble is that God, as a friend of mine once said, can seem like "a lot of nothing" and so cannot seem to rival the beauty I can see with my eyes. It is true, "Nothing disturb you, nothing affright you" can cast out fear only if you believe in the reality of God, and "Patience attains to all" only if you wait on the coming of God. Everything depends on a kindling of the heart.

Or we must, God must "rekindle hearts in a world that grow chill." Who must? Actually beauty, like goodness, is transcendental, as in Saint Augustine's famous exclamation, "Late have I loved you, beauty so old and so new: late have I loved you!"[40] And so Tolstoy's "delusion that beauty is goodness" is not such a delusion after all. No doubt there can be a delusion in not realizing the beauty that fascinates me is passing, but there is a beauty that is unchanging, and such beauty is goodness. Transcendental, nevertheless, means universal like being and one and true and good. But this touches also on the passing as well as the unchanging and so places the passing in a different light. My own conclusion is that I must connect with the passing as well as with the unchanging.

Indeed one who connects with God is connecting with the passing as well as the unchanging. That is why "One who holds to God (or has God) lacks nothing." When Heidegger talks of Being he is speaking of the transcendental, and when Saint Teresa speaks of God, she is speaking of the transcendent. There is a connection, nevertheless, between the transcendental and the transcendent, the wonder of existence and the existence of God. As I understand it, Heidegger's concept of Being corresponds to Wittgenstein's concept of the mystical, not *how* things are but *that* they are, and that relates directly with the existence of God the creator. The difference between the passing and the unchanging is a difference in *how* things are, but one who connects with the wonder *that* things are lacks nothing.

So one who has God or holds to God, has or holds to the wonder of existence. "To have and to hold" does not work with beings, especially not with human beings, you have to let them go, but it can with Being and thus it can with God. Yet looking at it more closely, you can see the attitude towards God is the attitude towards Being, letting be and openness to the mystery. So holding to God means holding to letting go, a paradox, and having God means opennness to mystery that shows and withdraws. It is a holding that is a letting go and a having that is an openness. The essence of Being is letting be (*Gelassenheit*) as in "Let there be light," and so one who lets be and is open to the mystery lacks nothing. Thus

Solo Dios basta.   God alone is enough.

I think of the words over the entrance to the monastery of Gethsemane in Kentucky, "God alone." I think also of the prayer of Saint Ignatius ending "Give me your love and your grace, for this is enough for me."[41] Wisdom is knowing what is enough for you, I know, but I am afraid of saying that prayer, because there are many other things I desire. Is letting be and openness to mystery enough for me? There is peace in it, I can say, a peace of mind and heart and soul, and wholeness, learning to love with all your mind and with all your heart and with all your soul. Or that is how I see it, peace and wholeness, learning to love, and love of God, as I keep quoting from Spinoza, is simply joy at the thought of God. Letting be and openness to the mystery, as Heidegger understands it, is a relationship with technology, but as I understand it a relationship with others and with self and with God.

Letting be is doing what God is doing, as in "Let there be light." It is true, my letting be does not cause the world to exist as God's does. All the same, it does mean entering into and participating in God's relation with the world. I remember playing creation of the world when I was a child. What my game amounted to was letting everything be as in the story of the seven days in Genesis. Nowadays we play the game as adults with our scientific cosmology: we gaze at the stars, and we are looking into the past as light travels at a finite speed, and we think back to the beginning of time. Here again we come upon the mystical, "not *how* the world is but *that* it is," though scientific cosmology is about *how* the world is. Creation is not about *how* the world is, that it has a beginning in time, beginning say with a Big Bang, but is about Being, *that* the world exists.

Openness to the mystery then is openness to the mystery that shows and withdraws in the existence of the world, that shows and withdraws also in my own existence, the mystery that I am. I think again of Wittgenstein's sayings about the mystical, "Not *how* the world is, is the mystical, but *that* it is" and "The feeling of the world as a limited whole is the mystical feeling" and "There is indeed the inexpressible. This *shows* itself; it is the mystical." Is the mystical then enough for me? "Existence is God," Meister Eckhart says, *Esse est Deus,*[42] meaning the wonder of existence, and in that sense I could say the mystical is enough for me, the wonder of God showing and withdrawing in the existence of the world and in my own existence. It is God, though, who is enough for me, God alone, showing and withdrawing also in human relations.

"God is spirit" then and God is enough for me in that "It is the spirit that gives life; the flesh is of no avail."[43] I find it difficult, nevertheless, to embrace the life of spirit without reserve, without reserving the life of flesh. Still, "Seek peace and ensue it"[44] is the imperative of my life and guides me into the life of spirit, into hope and peace and friends and intelligence, into life and light and love. I can see the truth of it, hope and peace and friends and intelligence are enough for me, life and light and love are enough for me. There is an illumining of my mind and a kindling of my heart in this. Hope and peace and friends and intelligence are the life of the spirit. Life and light and love are eternal life.

The Practice of the Presence

And I said to the man who stood at the gate of the year, Give me a light that I may tread safely into the unknown. And he replied, Go out into the darkness and put your hand into the hand of God. That shall be to you better than light and safer than a known way.

—M. L. Haskins quoted by George VI

◆ "Beyond logic, beyond reason, beyond hope. Trust me," the words of the High One in Patricia McKillip's *Riddle Master,* and "Go out into the darkness and put your hand into the hand of God," the words of the man who stood at the gate of the year in M. Louise Haskins' poem,[1] are a guide to the practice of the presence. Striving doesn't work, I learned when I was in the novitiate, trying to practice the presence of God on a cold winter's day, as we worked in silence, tending grapevines, and I was drawing a blank. Striving doesn't work but instead you have to trust, "Trust me" and "put your hand into the hand of God."

"God requires the heart," as is said in the Talmud, and that, as I understand it, means trust in God and willingness to follow God's guidance. Faith, it seems, is just this combination of willingness and hope. The classical discussion of this is Kierkegaard's in *Fear and Trembling* where he compares and contrasts "the knight of faith" who has willingness and hope and "the knight of infinite resignation" who has willingness but without hope. Kierkegaard is working here from the story of Abraham, but we could take the story as one of the presence of God as well as one of faith. One of the problems Kierkegaard sees in reflecting on the story of Abraham is Abraham's silence. It is a silence in response to the presence, as if the presence of God were something of which one cannot speak. I think of Wittgenstein's concluding sentence in his *Tractatus*, "Whereof one cannot speak, thereof one must be silent."[2] I put this together with his statements about the mystical, especially the last, "There is indeed the inexpressible. This *shows* itself; it is the mystical."

As I reflect on Wittgenstein's silence, I think of Shakespeare, who kept silence on the religious issues of his day. On the other hand, I think of Saint Augustine, who speaks in the presence of God in his *Confessions*. Perhaps it is like "catching the light": though we do not see the light by itself, we see things *in* the light. So too we can speak *in* the presence of God, we can pray, that is, even if the presence itself is elusive, "shows itself," as Wittgenstein says of the mystical, "and at the same time withdraws," as Heidegger says of the mystery. Thus Abraham speaks *in* the presence of God in the story told in Genesis, though he keeps silence before others, and he is always making covenants with God, relying on God's promises.

A practice of the presence of God, therefore, is a way of relating to the presence showing and withdrawing. "What *can* be shown *cannot* be said,"[3] Wittgenstein says, making his distinction between saying and showing. "The meaning pervading technology hides itself," Heidegger says, "we stand at once within the realm of that which hides itself from us, and hides itself just in approaching us."[4] The presence of God, I want to say, is just such a meaning, just such a mystery, and we practice the presence of God by letting things be and being open to the mystery that is showing and withdrawing in them. That is the conclusion we come to on our vision quest, I believe, letting be and openness to the mystery.

There are three riddles unanswered in our time that need to be answered in a vision:

(A) Dark Matter,
(B) Eternal Life,
and (C) "How can the knower be known?"

Dark matter is a riddle that has come up in modern scientific cosmology, the presence of matter in the universe which cannot be directly observed but is inferred from its gravitational effects on the stars. Eternal life is the riddle of life after death, again something we cannot directly observe but something we can infer from the deeper life of the spirit already begun in this world. And "How can the knower be known?" is the riddle that is posed in the Upanishads,[5] again a matter not of direct knowing but of inference from the knowing that we do have. The indirection in these riddles is like that in "catching the light": we do not see the light but we see things *in* the light. And so it is with these riddles: we do not see dark matter but we see things situated by dark matter; we do not see life after death but we see a deeper life now that can live on; and we do not see the knower but we see things known by the knower.

Are these riddles connected with the presence showing and withdrawing in the world? Matter is a dimension, I want to say, like space and time. I know this is not an accepted idea, for I wrote years ago to Schrödinger, who worked out wave mechanics, asking him about it, and received a one sentence reply, "Matter is *not* a dimension."[6] I have returned to the idea, nevertheless, these many years later, matter not only situated but also situating. Dark matter for instance is only discernible by its gravitational effects, i.e., by its situating. And if we say matter is a dimension along with space and time, then what is *in* the dimensions? Events, I want to say, even the showing and withdrawing of mystery or of the presence. What is more, matter situates life and intelligence, and thus the brain is not the mind but situates the mind.

Words and music, we have been saying, are connected with the left and right sides of the brain and in turn with the right hand and the left hand. Wittgenstein has it that "a right hand glove could be put on the left hand if it could be turned around in four-dimensional space."[7] My own solution is simply to turn the glove inside out. Adding a dimension and turning around is equivalent, that is, to turning inside out, and thus adding the dimension of matter and turning around is equivalent to turning space-time inside out. If words are music inside out and music words inside out, as I have been saying, matter situates the words and the music, the musical instrument situates the music, for instance the harp. But the human voice too is a musical instrument and situates words and music in song, and the human body situates them in dance.

Matter situates, that is what I mean by saying matter is a dimension like space and time, and if I say this I mean to leave the door open to spirit. I want to leave the door open to the life of the spirit, hope and peace and friends and intelligence, and I want to leave the door open to God, as "God is spirit." If we do not say matter is a dimension but say matter is what is *in* the dimensions of space and time, we are saying everything in space and time has to be material, and we will have to say with Wittgenstein "The solution of the riddle of life in space and time lies *outside* space and time" and "God does not reveal himself in the world."[8] As it is, though, the life of spirit, hope and peace and friends and intelligence, exists already in space and time, and God acts in space and time, illumining minds and kindling hearts.

If matter is a dimension, "Everything that exists is situated," as Max Jacob says in the preface to his poems in *The Dice Cup*, "Everything that's above matter is situated; matter itself is situated."[9] So there can be things above matter such as life and intelligence if matter is a dimension situating things. And besides existence there can be transcendence, something beyond space and time and matter, namely God, though God can act in the situated world. To practice the presence of God is to connect with transcendence in the midst of existence. And this is how the riddle of eternal life arises. If I connect with transcendence in the midst of my existence, if I pray or live a life of prayer, living in the standpoint before God, I may hope to connect with transcendence in death as well as in life, I may hope to survive death and live on in God.

> What can I know?
> What should I do?
> What may I hope?[10]

Kant's three questions come up here. All we can know from experience is life on this side of death, but if eternal life begins already on this side as the life of spirit, then we can know eternal life too. I keep describing the life of spirit as "hope and peace and friends and intelligence." Can that life survive death? I suppose the essential thing is connecting with transcendence during my earthly existence, thus hope and peace and friends and intelligence in relation with God. I think that is what is meant by "eternal life" in the Gospel of John, hope or trust in God, and the peace of God, and friends in God, and intelligence or wisdom of God, what we can know in the standpoint of prayer. "And this is eternal life, that they know thee the only true God, and Jesus Christ whom thou hast sent,"[11] knowing God, I take it, by entering into the relationship of Jesus with his God, "my Father and your Father," as he says to Mary Magdalene, "my God and your God."

What then should I do? "Only connect!" as E. M. Forster says, connect with others, connect with myself, connect with God. How to connect, though, is the question. If the love of God is simply joy at the thought of God, as Spinoza says, joy at the thought of being on a journey with God, as I want to say, joy at the thought of God being with me, then it is out of joy that I am to relate to others and to myself. That means relating out of fullness rather than emptiness. I know what it is to relate out of emptiness, out of sadness and loneliness. To relate out of fullness is like restringing a harp that has been tuned to sorrow, returning the strings to joy. "Its strings were tuned to his sorrow, and its wood split like his heart," the harpist says in Patricia McKillip's story. "I strung my harp with them, matching note for note in the restringing. And then I returned them to my joy."[12]

What then may I hope? If my life is a journey in time and God is my companion on the way, I live in what Meister Eckhart calls "a wandering joy" on "the wayless way, where the children of God lose themselves and, at the same time, find themselves."[13] Christ is that way insofar as I walk with his God, "my Father and your Father," as he says to me too, "my God and your God." Here then is the riddle of eternal life in the form of a riddle game, the question: Who was Enoch? the answer: "Enoch walked with God; and he was not, for God took him," and the stricture, or the moral of the story: Walk on! My hope, then, is eternal life, walking with God.

More light on eternal life comes from answering the question of the Upanishads, "How can the knower be known?" I cannot leap over my own shadow, and that is an image of the mystery I am to myself, and if I am a mystery to myself, the meaning of my life "shows itself" to me "and at the same time withdraws" from me. No doubt, eternal life belongs to the mystery, How can I, the knower, be known to myself? "I do not know myself," Goethe says, "and God forbid that I should."[14] Being unknown to myself, I long to be known by another. "There is no one here who has an understanding for me in full," Kafka writes in his diary. "To have even one who had this understanding, for instance a woman, would be to have support from every side. It would be to have God."[15] How then can the knower be known by another? Loneliness, I can see, is this longing to be known by another, to have someone "who has an understanding for me in full." And to have this understanding, I can see, "would be to have support from every side," "to have God." How is it possible, though, to put the question in Kantian form, for one human being to have an understanding for another in full?

When you do find someone who seems to understand you in full, you find it is not quite "in full" (*im ganzen*), a considerable requirement. Only God, it seems, can understand us in full. That is why to have someone who had this understanding would be indeed to have support from every side, to have God. "Only God enters into the soul" (*solus Deus illabitur animae*).[16] If then I let others off on this demand for full understanding, I have to live with the mystery I am to myself and/or turn to God for full understanding. I have to pray with Saint Augustine, "May I know me! May I know thee!" At the same time, I have to forgive others, to release them from my needs, my expectations of full understanding, to release them and thereby be released myself. Where does that leave me? Again, letting be and being open to the mystery.

"We are hindered by cleaving to time," Meister Eckhart says. "Whatever cleaves to time is mortal."[17] David Applebaum quotes this as the epigraph of his book *The Vision of Kant*. I suppose he has in mind what Kant calls "the transcendental," not God or the transcendent but the human mind prior to experience, the timelessness of concepts, though Kant believed concepts without experience are empty, and experience without concepts is blind. Anyway the real alternative to cleaving to time is cleaving to eternity, to the transcendent, to connect with God, and that is what I want to do, letting be and keeping open to the mystery. Eternal life, I want to say, belongs not to those who live in the timelessness of concepts, who act always on principle, but to those who live in the presence, who live in the wandering joy of a journey with God.

One who has let go, who is heart-free, Meister Eckhart says, "experiences such a joy that no one would be able to tear it away." But such a one, being detached, "remains unsettled," he says, is ever on a journey. One who has let oneself be, and who has let God be, "lives in a wandering joy, or joy without a cause."[18] Here is the meaning of letting be and openness to the mystery, letting other persons be but also letting oneself be and letting God be, and living in the joy of being on a journey, an adventure, with God as one's companion on the way. It is "joy without a cause" insofar as the joy of being with God on an adventure is just that and doesn't depend on what happens in the course of the journey, and thus it is "such a joy that no one would be able to tear it away."

At the bottom of letting be and openness to the mystery is "the transcendence of longing,"[19] our heart's longing always going beyond any finite object. Thus it leads to disappointment to set your heart on someone or something finite, and if you wish to have a lasting relationship it has to be a journey *with* rather than *towards* the other. Letting myself be and letting God be is letting God reveal God to me and letting God reveal me to me, letting God answer the prayer "May I know me! May I know thee!" The transcendence of longing is the thing in us that corresponds to the transcendence of God. Openness to the mystery showing and withdrawing is openness to this elusive transcendence in us and in God.

If "our heart is restless until it rests in you," as Saint Augustine says, and if "the heart has reasons that reason does not know,"[20] as Pascal says, then the transcendental, the true transcendental, more than the structures Kant describes, is this transcendence of longing. Insight, I want to say, is what happens when reasons of the heart become known to the mind. "If, as Kierkegaard writes, longing alone is not sufficient for salvation," Adorno says, "still the images of beauty devolve upon longing through which the course of deliverance, disappearing, must travel if it is ever to lead to landing and awakening."[21] The restlessness of desire is a restless movement from image to image of beauty. To come to rest in God, Adorno is saying, I must go through that restless movement. I must come to rest in restlessness, I would say, to accept my own restlessness, that is, and thus I will come to repose in God, to repose in "a center of stillness surrounded by silence."

"We all have within us a center of stillness surrounded by silence," Hammarskjöld's words introducing the Meditation Room at the UN, speak to me of the presence of God as a surrounding silence. Or I interpret the surrounding silence as the presence of God. From a Buddhist standpoint of meditation the silence is simply the silence. From a Christian standpoint of prayer, however, the silence can be taken as the surrounding presence of God. If "our heart is restless until it rests in you," our heart finds rest in our center of stillness, and if "the heart has reasons that reason does not know," these reasons become known to the mind when we are in our center of stillness, and we must come into our center in order to know the reasons of the heart. "Faith is God sensible to the heart,"[22] Pascal says in that same context, and I take it God is sensible as a "stillness surrounded by silence."

"Be still and know that I am God"[23] it is said in the psalm, and it is by being still, I want to say, that we know God. What we know by being still is the peace of God; we know it as an inner peace. Where God is there is peace, and where peace is there is God. In a story of becoming a tree it is said "You must simply learn to be still."[24] Learning the presence of God is that too, learning to be still. I think again of Pascal saying all our troubles stem from our inability to sit quietly in a room, and Kafka saying if we could only sit still the world would offer itself to us. Becoming a tree, or becoming like a tree, is practicing the same stillness outdoors, no longer quietly in a room but in the open. I think of walking in the quiet and stillness of the giant redwoods. There again I am walking, not sitting, walking in the presence, walking with God. I think of Meister Eckhart saying that along the pathway of life all things speak, and in what remains unsaid in their speech "there is God, only God."[25]

A vision quest, like the traditional one of solitary vigil to seek spiritual power and to learn through a vision the identity of a guardian spirit, is fulfilled in a practice of the presence of God. For me it is coming to see my life as a journey in time and God as my companion on the way. Waiting on God is my solitary vigil, waiting on the illumining of the mind and the kindling of the heart; the power to become a friend and companion of God is the spiritual power I seek; and God is my guardian spirit, "my Father and your Father," as Christ says to Mary Magdalene, "my God and your God." A vision then it is of a great circle, of coming from God and returning to God with God at my side, as in the story "Enoch walked with God; and he was not, for God took him." In the words of the old Bedouin to Lawrence of Arabia, "the love is from God and of God and towards God." There you have it, all my favorite sayings.

Inside out, my answer to the Kantian dilemma of the right hand and the left hand, is part of the vision, words going with the left brain and the right hand, music with the right brain and the left hand, words as music inside out and music as words inside out, just as a right hand glove turned inside out fits the left hand and vice versa a left hand glove inside out fits the right hand. What does inside out mean of words and music? Well, to me it means the musical origin of language, and on the other hand the linguistic origin of music. "He believed, like Vico, that the world's first languages were in song," Bruce Chatwin says in *The Songlines* of a Chinese musical scholar and village schoolmaster "who lived with his childlike wife in a wooden house beside the Jade Stream."[26] Inscape, I gather, is the inside of words, and rhythm is the element common to words and music. Gerard Manley Hopkins writing of inscape and of rhythm, I think, is where we would have to look for light on the inside out relation of words and music.

> Look at the stars! Look, look up at the skies!
> O look at all the fire-folk sitting in the air!

he writes of the wonder of existence, looking up into night sky.[27]

"Tom sang most of the time," Tolkien writes of Tom Bombadil, "but it was chiefly nonsense, or else perhaps a strange language unknown to the hobbits, an ancient language whose words were mainly those of wonder and delight."[28] That is how I imagine the world's first languages in song, when early humanity, as the Chinese village schoolmaster believed, "had lived in musical harmony with the rest of Creation." I envision thus an original harmony, and then a disruption of the harmony with the emergence and separation of the human race into peoples at war and at peace, then the emergence and separation of the individual human being in loneliness, and finally and still to come a reunion with humanity and with God on the mystic road of love, "the road of the union of love with God."

I think again in conclusion of the words of a Chinese grandmother, a concert pianist, to one of my former students, Heather Hue, who was practicing a difficult Chopin nocturne on the piano and became frustrated and was banging on the piano. "You must love the music, not master it," her Chinese grandmother said quietly, coming up behind her. "Music must be treated as all things that are eternal, such as love and understanding, because it is these things that will carry us through the darkness of our lives and the death of our bodies to the moon of everlasting peace."[29]

A Vision Quest:
Song and Dance Cycle

Vigil
We keep
our solitary vigil,
watching
and waiting for our God.

A Vision of Emanation
One
and from the One the Many
in cascading radiations,
first Mind (Let there be light!)
then Soul (Let there be life!)
then Body (Let there be love!)
—we experience
our consciousness
but as an emanation
of creating impulse
that is ruling all the world
and drawing back
the Many to the One.

**"Whereof one cannot speak
thereof one must be silent"**
Our story is told and untold,
for I can tell the story
of my learning how to love
with all my mind in peaceful
   vision,
all my heart in facing death,
all my soul in lack and loss and
   letting go,
all my might in song and
   dance,
and yet the story of a soul
wandering away from God
and then in torment and in
   tears
finding its way home
through conversion
is the story told by saints
of all the world.

Music and Memory
There is a harmony
of all the universe,
and you can hear it
in our harmony,
the inscape of our language
and the origin of words,
for much we cannot say
only because the name it has
does not occur to us,
for we forget the song
that gives the names,
a song to remember
our forgetfulness
of things past and to come.

Time and Memory
My song then is of time,
a changing image of eternity,
a missing link
in our space theory of matter
where curvature is passed
along from place to place
as wave and particle
—I sing of a distension of the
    soul
where there is dancing,
where there is the way
of insight into image
of horizons circled,
letting be
and openness to mystery.

The Beginning of Time
In the beginning

God was sowing the seeds,
the seminal reasons
for everything that exists,
so in our beginning is our end
and in our end is our beginning,
for our reasons of being
are seminal
like rose hips
or buttercup achenes,
and so we do become
what we are indeed
as in the maxim,
Become what you are!

Equinox
We dance
a leaping spring,
a gentle fall
of our bright year in the
    woods.

A Vision of Evolution
Chance is a name
for our unknowing,
and natural selection too,
as chance survival,
is a name to name
the cloud of our unknowing
where we are oned
with God who draws life
out of matter
and intelligence
out of life,
having sown the seeds
in the beginning
and harvesting all in the end.

Alpha
Light comes in time
from many worlds ago,
I learned in boyhood
as I lay looking up
into the summer night
—there is a hemisphere
we see and one beyond
event horizons
where light is a point
that is the Alpha,
the beginning
of the mystical,
not only *how* things are
but *that* they are and *I am.*

Evolution of Matter
All in heaven
and on earth is situated,
all except the One,
and matter also situates,
like space and time
dimensional,
the body situates the soul,
the brain the mind.
Only the One
transcends,
only the longing,
heart's desire,
and everything that rises
must converge.

Evolution of Life
There is beauty
in the double helix,

secret of our origin,
but there is ugliness
in struggle for existence
and survival of the fittest—
Where is God's hand in all this?
A Sower went out to sow
and as he broadcast the seed
some fell along the way,
some on the rocky soil,
some in among the thorns,
and some upon the good earth
and its yield was manifold.

Evolution of Intelligence
Words and music
come together in the songs
of our first languages,
words rising
from our left brain,
music rising
from our right brain,
as if words were music
inside out just as a glove
made for the right hand
fits the left turned inside out,
emerged and separated
as we are,
inscape is music of our words.

Omega
I have found the joy
of a mystic road of love,
a road that makes of death
a fulfilment of your life,
a road of the heart's desire

that goes on ever on
and does not deadend
in a heat death of the world
—it is the one through road,
and running like a river,
its springs at every doorstep,
every path its tributary,
is the road of union
of all love in love of God.

Sun Dance
O let the sun
dance our passing,
and dancing too
we'll fear then no more.

A Great Circle
If the love is from God
and of God and towards God,
as the old man of the desert
said to Lawrence at the well,
we all live in a circle,
a great circle of the love,
of life and light and love,
as in the words of eternal life
where Jesus comes from God
and then returns to God,
and we too come and go
to my Father and your Father,
as Jesus says to Magdalene,
to my God and your God,
for love is from God
and of God and towards God.

Kindling Heart's Desire
We all have
inscape in us
that is in no other,
but this inner landscape
is revealed to us
only if we feel
our strongest feeling,
wish our central wish,
and stir the heart's desire
that stirs our inmost being,
for we listen
to our inmost selves
and do not know the music
we hear murmuring.

Heat Death
There is a heat death
of the spirit,
like the heat death
of the universe,
but God is spirit
and the fire of spirit
cannot ever die,
and God is able
to sustain our hope and
peace and friends and
    intelligence,
warming us
in fires of creation
as our human world
is growing chill.

Rekindling Hearts
Bright is the ring of words
if you can ring their music,
for our labors are of love
and understanding,
and the music of the words
will heal all
weariness of spirit,
and you may rekindle hearts
in a world that grows chill,
but as for me,
my heart is with the sea
of infinite substance
that God is,
and I listen for its singing.

An Eternal Vision
We have in us
a center of repose
that is surrounded
by a singing silence
that is presence,
a quiet eye
of storm,
heart's rest
upon the boundless
sea of God,
always with us,
a life's companion
on my life's
uncertain voyage.

Illumining Minds
Attention
like deep harmony
is prayer,
and listening to God
the restless sea
and to God's singing
of our coming
and our going,
we find rest
in restlessness
and tell sea tales
of our adventures,
knowing we know
more than we can tell.

Circle Dance
("Weave a circle round him thrice."
　　　—Coleridge, Kubla Khan)

We dance
a circle here now
around a center
that is everywhere.

Notes

Preface

    1. George Eliot, *Middlemarch* (Oxford: Oxford University Press, 1996), p. 182 (chap. 20).

    2. Teilhard de Chardin quoted by Flannery O'Connor, *Everything that Rises Must Converge* (New York: Farrar, Straus & Giroux, 1991).

    3. T. E. Lawrence, *Seven Pillars of Wisdom* (Harmondsworth, UK: Penguin and Jonathan Cape, 1971), p. 864. See my discussion in *Reasons of the Heart* (New York: Macmillan, 1978; rpt. Notre Dame, Ind.: University of Notre Dame Press, 1979), p. 1.

    4. Michael Polanyi, *The Tacit Dimension* (New York: Doubleday/Anchor, 1967), p. 4.

    5. Ascribed to Aquinas in George N. Shuster, *Saint Thomas Aquinas* (New York: Heritage, 1971), p. 3. See my discussion in *Reading the Gospel* (Notre Dame, Ind.: University of Notre Dame Press, 2000), p. ix.

    6. Inayat Khan (1882–1927) quoted by Bob Snyder as the epigraph of his book *Music and Memory* (Cambridge, Mass.: MIT Press, 2000), p. xiii.

A Vision Quest

    1. Martin Heidegger, *Poetry, Language, Thought*, trans. Albert Hofstadter (New York: Harper & Row, 1971), p. 4.

    2. J. R. R. Tolkien, *The Lord of the Rings*, one volume edition (London: George Allen & Unwin, 1976), p. 286.

    3. Mary Stewart, *Merlin Trilogy* (New York: William Morrow, 1980), p. 910.

4. T. E. Lawrence, *Seven Pillars of Wisdom* (Harmondsworth, UK: Penguin & Jonathan Cape, 1971), p. 364. See my discussion in my *Reasons of the Heart*, p. 1.

5. Ludwig Wittgenstein, *Tractatus Logico-Philosophicus,* trans. D. F. Pears and B. F. McGuinness (London: Routledge & Kegan Paul, 1961), p. 149 (#6.45).

6. Walter Van Tilburg Clark, *The Watchful Gods and Other Stories* (New York: Random House, 1950). Thales is quoted in Aristotle's *De Anima* 411a8.

7. *The Cloud of Unknowing and Other Works,* trans. Clifton Wolters (New York: Penguin, 1978), p. 46 (the original title).

8. Ibid., p. 211 (phrase from "Dionysius' Mystical Teaching" trans. by the author of *The Cloud*).

9. Abraham Pais, *"Subtle Is the Lord . . ."* (Oxford: Oxford University Press, 1982).

10. Robert Bolt, *A Man for All Seasons* (New York: Vintage, 1962), p. 38.

11. Charles Darwin, Letter to J. D. Hooker, 13 July 1856, in Frederick Burkhardt and Sydney Smith, eds., *The Correspondence of Charles Darwin,* vol. 6 (Cambridge: Cambridge University Press, 1990), p. 178.

12. Genesis 1:10, 12, 18, 21 and 25 (also 4 and 31) (RSV).

13. Saint Thomas Aquinas, *Summa Theologiae,* part 1, question 5, article 3 in his *Opera Omnia* (New York: Musurgia, 1948), vol. 1, pp. 18–19.

14. See my discussion of this saying in my *Church of the Poor Devil* (New York: Macmillan, 1982; rpt. Notre Dame: University of Notre Dame Press, 1983), p. 111.

15. Flannery O'Connor, *Mystery and Manners,* ed. Sally and Robert Fitzgerald (New York: Farrar, Straus & Giroux, 1969), p. 226. See my discussion in my *Church of the Poor Devil,* p. 102.

16. Pais, *"Subtle Is the Lord . . . ,"* p. vii.

17. Tennessee Williams, *Plays 1957–1980,* vol. 2 (New York: Library of America, 2000), p. 107.

18. Plautus, The Comedy of Asses (Asinaria), line 495 in *Plautus,* trans. Paul Nixon (Cambridge, Mass.: Harvard University Press, 1997), vol. 1, p. 176.

19. Joseph Conrad, *Heart of Darkness* (New York: Penguin, 1982), pp. 99–100.

20. Marcel Proust, *A la récherché du temps perdu,* vol. 1 (Paris: Gallimard, 1954), p. 100. See my discussion in my *Reasons of the Heart*, p. 71.

21. Proust, *A la récherché*, vol. 4 (Paris: Gallimard, 1989), p. 449 (*Les vrais paradis sont les paradis qu'on a perdus*).
22. Martin Heidegger, *Discourse on Thinking*, trans. John M. Anderson and E. Hans Freund (New York: Harper & Row, 1966), p. 55.
23. Luke 20:38 (RSV).
24. Plotinus, *Enneads* 6:9, in A. H. Armstrong, ed., *Plotinus*, vol. 7 (Cambridge, Mass.: Harvard University Press, 1988), p. 344 (*monos pros monon*). Armstrong translates "in solitude to the solitary." See my discussion in my *Mystic Road of Love* (Notre Dame: University of Notre Dame Press, 1999), p. 50.
25. Tolkien, *The Lord of the Rings*, p. 988.
26. Mimi Louise Haskins as quoted by George VI in a Christmas broadcast in 1939, *King George VI to His Peoples* (London: John Murray, 1952), p. 21. See my use of these words in my *Love's Mind* (Notre Dame: University of Notre Dame Press, 1993), p. 66 and *Reading the Gospel*, p. 58.
27. Patricia McKillip, *Riddle-Master* (New York: Ace, 1999), p. 179.
28. John 4:24 (RSV).
29. Wittgenstein, *Tractatus Logico-Philosphicus*, trans. C. K. Ogden (New York: Dover, 1999), p. 107 (6.44, 6.45, and 6.522).
30. Tolkien, *The Lord of the Rings*, p. 1100.
31. John 20:17 (RSV).
32. See my discussion of this saying from the Talmud in my *Peace of the Present* (Notre Dame: University of Notre Dame Press, 1991), p. 18, and *Reading the Gospel*, p. 84.
33. Exodus 33:14 (RSV).

The Riddle of Eternal Life

1. "I am my world" in Wittgenstein, *Tractatus Logico-Philosophicus* (trans. Ogden), p. 89 (#5.63). "Am I my time?" in Heidegger, *The Concept of Time*, trans. William McNeill (Oxford, UK and Cambridge, USA: Blackwell, 1992), p. 22 E.
2. Geoffrey Chaucer, *Canterbury Tales*, The Wife of Bath's Prologue, line 473 in *The Poetical Works of Chaucer*, ed. F. N. Robinson (Boston: Houghton Mifflin, 1933), p. 96.
3. Isak Dinesen, *Last Tales* (New York: Random House, 1957), p. 26.
4. Michael Polanyi, *The Tacit Dimension*, p. 4.

5. Here I am using the translation of Wittgenstein's *Tractatus* by D. F. Pears and B. F. McGuinness as above in "A Vision Quest" (note 5), p. 147 (#6.4311). See my discussion in my book *Reading the Gospel*, p. 116.

6. Henry Vaughan, "The World" in Robert Penn Warren and Albert Erskine, eds., *Six Centuries of Great Poetry* (New York: Bantam Doubleday Dell, 1955), p. 271.

7. Wendell Berry, "Setting Out" in *The Wheel* (San Francisco: North Point, 1982), p. 26.

8. Henry Vaughan, "They Are All Gone into the World of Light" in *Six Centuries of Great Poetry*, p. 276.

9. See my *Mystic Road of Love*, "A Note on the Dante-Riemann Universe," pp. 137–141.

10. William Wordsworth, "Preface to Lyrical Ballads" in *William Wordsworth*, ed. Stephen Gill (Oxford: Oxford University Press, 1990), p. 611.

11. Dante uses the phrase *alta fantasia* in the very last canto, *Paradiso*, canto 33, line 142.

12. Chaucer, "Truth: Balade de Bon Conseyle," line 1, in *The Poetical Works of Chaucer*, p. 631.

13. Shakespeare, *As You Like It*, act 2, scene 7, line 139. See below note 14.

14. Matthew 7:1 (RSV).

15. See Richard Knowles, ed., *As You Like It* (New York: Modern Language Association of America, 1977), p. 130, note.

16. John 6:68 (RSV).

17. Augustine, *Soliloquies*, bk. 2, chap. 1 (my translation). See my discussion in *A Search for God in Time and Memory* (New York: Macmillan, 1969; rpt. Notre Dame: University of Notre Dame Press, 1977) p. 52, and *Love's Mind*, p. 61.

18. John 17:3 (RSV).

19. Augustine, *Retractations*, bk. 1, chap. 4, trans. John H. S. Burleigh in *Augustine: Earlier Writings* (Philadelphia: Westminster, 1953), p. 18.

20. Shakespeare, *The Tempest*, act 1, scene 2, lines 49f. See my discussion in *A Search for God in Time and Memory*, p. 211.

21. Augustine, *Soliloquies*, bk. 2, chap. 1, trans. Burleigh in *Augustine: Earlier Writings*, p. 41.

22. Here I am using again Ogden's translation of Wittgenstein's *Tractatus*, p. 106 (#6.4312).

23. Augustine, *Confessions*, bk. 1, chap. 1, trans. Henry Chadwick (Oxford: Oxford University Press, 1991), p. 3.

24. See my *Reading the Gospel*, p. 143.

25. "Everyman" in *Earlier English Drama*, ed. F. J. Tickner (London: Nelson, 1926), p. 240. Genesis 5:24 (RSV)(Enoch).

26. See my discussion in *The Mystic Road of Love*, p. 91.

27. 2 Samuel 6:14 (RSV). The command to love "with all your heart, and with all your soul, and with all your might" is in Deuteronomy 6:4 (RSV). See Matthew 22:37, Mark 12: 29–30, and Luke 10:27 (RSV), adding "with all your mind."

28. Luke 10:25 (RSV).

29. W. H. Auden, "In Memory of W. B. Yeats" in *The Collected Poetry of W. H. Auden* (New York: Random House, 1945), p. 50.

30. Martin Buber, *I and Thou*, trans. Ronald Gregor Smith (New York: Scribner's, 1958), epigraph.

31. Luke 10:28 (RSV).

32. Psalm 23 (KJ).

33. See my *Mystic Road of Love*, pp. 88–89, 137, 154n55.

34. Wittgenstein, *Tractatus* (Ogden), p. 106 (#6.4311).

35. Heidegger, *Being and Time*, trans. John Macquarrie and Edward Robinson (New York: Harper & Row, 1962), p. 19.

36. Heidegger, *The Concept of Time*, pp. 1E–2E.

37. Ibid., p. 5E.

38. Heidegger's preface to William J. Richardson, *Heidegger: Through Phenomenology to Thought* (The Hague: M. Nijhoff, 1963), p. xx. See my discussion in *The Homing Spirit* (New York: Crossroad, 1987; rpt. Notre Dame: University of Notre Dame Press, 1997), p. 17.

39. Aquinas, *Summa Theologiae*, part 2/2, question 83, article 1 in *Opera Omnia* (reprint Musurgia), vol. 3, pp. 295–296.

40. Augustine, *Confessions*, bk. 11, chap. 14, trans. Chadwick, p. 230.

41. Ibid., chap. 26, p. 240. See James J. O'Donnell's commentary in his *Augustine: Confessions* (Oxford: Clarendon, 1992), vol. 3, pp. 289–290.

42. Shakespeare, Sonnets 30:2 and 107:2 in *The Pelican Shakespeare*, ed. Alfred Harbage (Baltimore: Penguin, 1969), p. 1458 and p. 1471. See my discussion in *The Homing Spirit*, p. 19.

43. Bertrand Russell, *Human Knowledge: Its Scope and Limits* (New York: Simon & Schuster, 1948), p. 123. Kurt Gödel, "A Remark about the Relationship between Relativity Theory and Idealistic Philosophy" in Paul Arthur Schilpp, ed., *Albert Einstein: Philosopher-Scientist* (Evanston, Ill.: Library of Living Philosophers, 1949), pp. 557–562. Ludwig Wittgenstein,

Philosophical Investigations, trans. G. E. M. Anscombe, 3rd ed. (New York: Macmillan, 1968), p. 42 (#89).

44. Marcel Proust, *Remembrance of Things Past,* vol. 2 "The Past Recaptured," trans. by Frederick A. Blossom, pp. 1123–1124.

45. Ibid., p. 1115.

46. Søren Kierkegaard, *Fear and Trembling* (with *Sickness unto Death*), trans. Walter Lowrie (Garden City, N.Y.: Doubleday, 1954), p. 30. It is in *Sickness unto Death* that he uses the phrase "an eternal self" as a kind of keyword.

47. Proust, *Remembrance of Things Past,* vol. 2, p. 996.

48. John 11:25–26 (RSV). See my first book, *The City of the Gods* (New York: Macmillan, 1965; rpt. Notre Dame: University of Notre Dame Press, 1978) at the end, p. 230.

49. Buber, *I and Thou,* pp. 66–67.

50. Heidegger, *Discourse on Thinking,* p. 85.

51. The one translation is Ogden's; the other is that of Pears and McGuinness, of proposition #6.4311 in the *Tractatus.*

52. Dag Hammarskjöld, *Markings,* trans. Leif Sjöberg and W. H. Auden (New York: Ballantine, 1985), p. 74.

53. Boethius, *The Consolation of Philosophy,* trans. W. V. Cooper (New York: Random House Modern Library, 1943), p. 115 (bk. 5).

54. Ibid., p. 26 (bk. 2).

55. Friedrich Nietzsche, *Thus Spake Zarathustra,* trans. Thomas Common, ed. Manuel Komroff (New York: Tudor, 1928), pp. 350–351.

56. Alan Lightman, *Einstein's Dreams* (New York: Pantheon, 1993), p. 52.

57. T. S. Eliot, *Four Quartets* (San Diego: Harcourt Brace Jovanovich, 1988), pp. 23 and 32 (the opening and closing lines of "East Coker").

58. Andrew Marvell, "To His Coy Mistress," in *Six Centuries of Great Poetry,* p. 258.

59. Wittgenstein, *Philosophical Investigations,* p. 97 (#281). Peter Hacker says "This epitomizes the conclusions we shall reach in our investigation" in his unpublished manuscript.

60. See my discussion in my *Mystic Road of Love* in the appendix "A Note on the Dante-Riemann Universe," pp. 137–141.

61. See the chapter "A Memory Theatre" in my *Music of Time,* (Notre Dame: University of Notre Dame Press, 1996), pp. 8–32.

62. Mircea Eliade, *Yoga: Immortality and Freedom,* trans. Willard R. Trask (Princeton, N.J.: Princeton University Press, 1969), pp. 241–243 (the bodily centers in Hinduism) and p. 410 (in Hesychasm).

63. Richard Crashaw, *The Religious Poems of Richard Crashaw*, ed. R. A. Eric Shepherd (St. Louis: Herder, 1914), p. 127 ("Temperance").
64. Augustine, *Confessions*, bk. 10, chap. 1 (Chadwick, p. 179).
65. Ibid., chap. 17 (Chadwick, p. 194).
66. Jonathan D. Spence, *The Memory Palace of Matteo Ricci* (New York: Penguin, 1985).
67. Michael S. Gazzaniga, *The Mind's Past* (Berkeley: University of California Press, 1998), p. 63.
68. T. S. Eliot, *Four Quartets*, p. 55 ("Little Gidding," lines 156–159).
69. Wittgenstein, *Tractatus* (Ogden), p. 103 (#6.36111).
70. Bruce Chatwin, *The Songlines* (New York: Penguin, 1987), p. 176.
71. In my *Love's Mind*, p. 129.
72. Wittgenstein, *Philosophical Investigations*, pp. 15–16 (#32). The passage from Augustine's *Confessions* he quotes on p. 2 (#1) is from bk. 1, chap. 8 (Chadwick, p. 10).
73. Wittgenstein, *Tractatus* (Ogden), pp. 44–45 (#4.002).
74. See the interview with John Adams by Jonathan Cott, June 1985, with the compact disc recording of Adams' *Harmonielehre* (Nonesuch Digital, 1985). I speak of this in *Reading the Gospel*, p. 31.
75. Rainer Maria Rilke, *Stories of God*, trans. M. D. Herter Norton (New York: Norton, 1963), p. 29. I speak of this in *Love's Mind*, p. 53.
76. Wittgenstein, *Philosophical Investigations*, p. 94 (#268).
77. Psalm 49:4 (from the Liturgy of the Hours).
78. W. B. Yeats, *Collected Poems* (New York: Macmillan, 1972), p. 214 ("Among School Children").
79. Dante, *Paradiso* 3:85 in *Le Opere di Dante Alighieri*, ed. E. Moore and Paget Toynbee (Oxford: Oxford University Press, 1963), p. 107. See Matthew Arnold, "The Study of Poetry" in his *Selected Essays*, ed. Noel Annan (London: Oxford University Press, 1962), p. 56.
80. Dag Hammarskjöld, "A Room of Quiet" (New York: United Nations, 1971), opening sentence. See my *House of Wisdom* (San Francisco: Harper & Row, 1985; rpt. Notre Dame: University of Notre Dame Press, 1993), p. 4 and pp. 118–148.
81. Boston Women's Health Collective, *Our Bodies Ourselves* (Harmondsworth: Penguin, 1976/1984).
82. See Gazzaniga's first chapter, "The Fictional Self," in *The Mind's Past*, pp. 1–27.
83. 2 Timothy 1:12 (KJ and RSV).
84. William Wordsworth in *Six Centuries of Great Poetry*, p. 369.

"Riddling, perplexed, labyrinthical soul!"

1. J. R. R. Tolkien, *The Hobbit* (New York: Houghton Mifflin, 1997), the chapter "Riddles in the Dark," pp. 64–83.

2. George Lakoff and Rafael E. Nuñez, *Where Mathematics Comes From: How the Embodied Mind Brings Mathematics into Being* (New York: Basic Books, 2000).

3. John Donne, *The Major Works*, ed. John Carey (Oxford: Oxford University Press, 1990), p. 389 (from a sermon preached 25 January, 1629).

4. W. B. Yeats, "A Dialogue of Self and Soul" in *Collected Poems* (New York: Macmillan, 1956), p. 230. See my discussion in my *Reasons of the Heart*, pp. 72–78.

5. T. S. Eliot, *The Three Voices of Poetry* (New York: Cambridge University Press, 1954). See my discussion in my *Reading the Gospel*, p. 42.

6. William Wordsworth, *The Prelude*, ed. E. E. Reynolds (London: Macmillan, 1932), p. 72 (5:595–597).

7. Aristotle, *Poetics*, trans. Malcolm Heath (New York: Penguin, 1996), p. 16. On metaphor, ibid., p. 34. See the Greek text *Aristotelis de arte poetica liber*, ed. Rudolf Kassel (Oxford: Clarendon, 1965), p. 15 on poetry and history (1451b5–7), and p. 34 on metaphor (1457b6ff.).

8. Lakoff and Nuñez, *Where Mathematics Comes From*, p. 41.

9. Wittgenstein, *Tractatus* (Ogden), p. 89 (#5.63), and *Philosophical Investigations*, p. 178.

10. Donne, "A Hymn to God the Father" in *Major Works*, p. 333.

11. Donne, "Devotions upon Emergent Occasions" XVII in *Major Works*, p. 344 (I have quoted it in thought lines, as is often done).

12. William Harvey, *De Motu Cordis*, trans. Chauncey D. Leake (Springfield, Ill.: Charles C. Thomas, 1970), p. 5.

13. Charles Williams, *The Image of the City and Other Essays* (London: Oxford University Press, 1958), p. 81.

14. Donne, Holy Sonnet in *Major Works*, p. 177.

15. Max Jacob, *The Dice Cup*, ed. Michael Brownstein (New York: State University of New York Press, 1979), p. 7. See my discussion in *House of Wisdom*, pp. 111-112, and in *Love's Mind*, p. 77.

16. See Gazzaniga's discussion in *The Mind's Past*, p. 8.

17. John 3:8 (RSV).

18. Aquinas, *Summa Theologiae*, part 1, question 2, article 1 in *Opera Omnia* (reprint Musurgia), vol. 1, p. 8.

19. W. B. Yeats, *Per Amica Silentia Lunae,* an essay in two parts, *Anima Hominis* and *Anima Mundi,* in his *Mythologies* (New York: Macmillan, 1959), p. 345.

20. The music of the song is in my *Reading the Gospel,* pp. 26–27. On the world soul see Nicolas Cusanus, *Of Learned Ignorance,* trans. Germain Heron (New Haven, Conn.: Yale University Press, 1954), pp. 97–103.

21. Hermann Broch, *The Death of Virgil,* trans. Jean Starr Untermeyer (San Francisco: North Point, 1945), p. 482 (concluding sentence).

22. Shakespeare, Sonnets 30:2 and 107:1–2 cited above in "The Riddle of Eternal Life," note 41.

23. Wisdom 7:27 (RSV).

24. Henry Chadwick in his preface to his translation of Augustine's *Confessions,* p. xxiv.

25. Hammarskjöld, *Markings,* p. 73.

26. I am using the Greek text in *Plato's Seventh and Eighth Letters,* ed. by R. S. Bluck (Cambridge: Cambridge University Press, 1947), p. 53 (The Seventh Letter 342). See the translation by Walter Hamilton in Plato, *Phaedrus and the Seventh and Eighth Letters* (New York: Penguin, 1973), p. 157. But I have translated the nouns into participles: naming, expressing, imaging, knowing, and being.

27. Ursula LeGuin, *A Wizard of Earthsea* (Berkeley, Calif.: Parnassus, 1968), p. 185. See my discussion in *House of Wisdom,* p. 13.

28. John 17:23 (RSV).

29. Ascribed to Aquinas in George N. Shuster, *Saint Thomas Aquinas,* p. 3. See my discussion in my *Reading the Gospel,* p. ix, and in my *Road of the Heart's Desire* (Notre Dame: University of Notre Dame Press, 2002) in the chapter "The Music of Words" (p. 87) where I translate myself the words of Aquinas from his prologue to the Psalms, *hymnus est laus Dei com cantico,* "a hymn is praise of God with song," *canticum autem exultatio mentis de aeternis habita,* "but song is exultation of the mind upon eternal things," *prorumpens in vocem,* "breaking into sound" (or "voice").

30. The opening words of his Corpus Christi hymn *Pange Lingua,* my translation.

31. I set these words to music in *The Music of Time,* p. 113.

32. My translation in *The Music of Time,* pp. 107–108.

33. See the interview of John Adams by Jonathan Cott, June 1985, with the Compact Disc recording of his *Harmonielehre* (New York: Nonesuch Records, 1985).

34. John 6:63 (RSV).

35. 1 John 1:1 my trans. in *Reading the Gospel*, p. 23.

36. W. B. Yeats, *A Vision* (New York: Collier, 1966), p. 83. See my discussion in *The Music of Time*, p. 12.

37. See my discussion of *Symphony of Psalms* in my *Music of Time*, pp. 111–112 and of *Symphony of Sorrowful Songs*, pp. 134–135, and of *Harmonium* in my *Love's Mind*, p. 104.

38. John Henry Newman, *Prose and Poetry*, ed. George N. Shuster (New York: Allyn & Bacon, 1925), p. 116. See his *Apologia pro Vita Sua* (New York: Doubleday, 1989), p. 152.

39. Christopher Logue, *War Music* (London: Jonathan Cape, 1981).

40. Kierkegaard, *Sickness unto Death*, trans. Walter Lowrie with *Fear and Trembling*, p. 258.

41. Bruce Chatwin, *The Songlines*.

42. The song cycle is at the end of my book *Reading the Gospel*, pp. 141–146. The music for the opening song "In the Beginning" is there on pp. 26–27. The song given above in "The Riddle of Eternal Life" is also from this cycle.

43. In my *Love's Mind*, p. 136.

44. Saint Augustine, *Confessions* (Chadwick), pp. 207–208 (bk. 10, chap. 33). Plato, *Timaeus*, ed. and trans. John Warrington (London: Dent and New York: Dutton, 1965), p. 30 (37C on time) and pp. 26–27 (35B–36B on soul and harmonic intervals).

45. I have the melody in my *Love's Mind* on p. 48.

46. The last line of *Faust* (my trans.). See my discussion in *Music of Time*, p. 7.

47. Saint Augustine, *Confessions* (Chadwick), p. 304 (bk. 13, chap. 35).

"Tell me where all past years are"

1. Yeats quoted above in "Riddling, perplexed, labyrinthical soul!" note 19.

2. Rilke quoted above in "The Riddle of Eternal Life," note 74.

3. Tolkien, *Lord of the Rings*, p. 1122.

4. Saint Ignatius of Loyola, *Spiritual Exercises*, trans. John Morris, ed. Henry Keane (London: Burns Oates & Washbourne, 1952), pp. 115–123.

5. Ibid., p. 121.

6. Cf. Sartre's essay "Existentialism is a Humanism" in Walter Kaufmann, ed., *Existentialism from Dostoevsky to Sartre* (New York: Meridian,

1956), pp. 292ff. See my discussion in *A Search for God in Time and Memory,* pp. 122–125.

7. Hammarskjöld quoted above in "The Riddle of Eternal Life," note 79.

8. Patricia McKillip, *The Sorceress and the Cygnet* (New York: Ace, 1991), p. 224.

9. Lessing as quoted by Kierkegaard in *Concluding Unscientific Postscript,* trans. David Swenson and Walter Lowrie (Princeton, N.J.: Princeton University Press, 1964), p. 97.

10. See my discussion of this saying (from the screenplay of *Shadowlands*) in *Reading the Gospel,* p. 1.

11. Lessing as quoted by Einstein in Abraham Pais, *Subtle is the Lord . . .,* p. 468.

12. Isidore of Sevilled as quoted by Marc Sebanc in the epigraph to his story *Flight to Hollow Mountain* (Grand Rapids, Mich.: Eerdmans, 1996), p. i.

13. Michel Serres, *Genesis,* trans. Genevieve James and James Nielson (Ann Arbor, Mich.: University of Michigan Press, 1995), p. 138 (his conclusion). See J. R. R. Tolkien, *The Silmarillion,* ed. Christopher Tolkien (Boston: Houghton Mifflin, 1977), pp. 15–17, and C. S. Lewis, *The Magician's Nephew* (New York: Collier, Macmillan, 1955), pp. 98–115.

14. Leo Tolstoy, *Fables and Fairy Tales,* trans. Ann Dunnigan (New York: Signet/NAL, 1962), pp. 82–88.

15. Rilke, *Stories of God,* p. 48.

16. Ibid., p. 66.

17. Ibid., p. 50.

18. Robert Bolt, *A Man for All Seasons* (New York: Vintage/Random House, 1962), p. 38.

19. Rilke, *Stories of God,* p. 74.

20. Buber, *Ecstatic Confessions,* trans. Esther Cameron, ed. Paul Mendes-Flohr (San Francisco: Harper & Row, 1985), p. 11.

21. Rilke, *Stories of God,* p. 86.

22. Ibid., p. 89.

23. Ibid., p. 95.

24. Ibid., p. 126.

25. Saint Augustine, *Confessions* (Chadwick), p. 191 (bk. 10, chap. 14).

26. From George Herbert's poem "The Call," set to music by Ralph Vaughan Williams in his song cycle *Five Mystical Songs* (1911).

27. Tolkien, *Lord of the Rings,* p. 848.

28. Ibid., p. 87.

29. Psalm 138:8. I am quoting it from the Liturgy of the Hours and then from KJ and RSV.

30. Ursula LeGuin quoted above in "Riddling, perplexed, labyrinthical soul!" note 27.

31. Tolkien, *Lord of the Rings*, p. 73 (and p. 640).

32. Tolkien at the end of his essay "On Fairy Stories" in *The Tolkien Reader* (New York: Ballantine, 1991), p. 89.

33. Arthur J. Arberry, *The Koran Interpreted* (Oxford: Oxford University Press, 1964), pp. 35 (Sura 2), 182 and 184 (Sura 9), 531 and 533 and 534 (Sura 48). See my conversation with David Daube on the Shekinah and the "I am" sayings of Jesus in my *Peace of the Present*, pp. 93–95.

34. John 16:28–29 (RSV).

35. Psalm 22:1 in Matthew 27: 46 and Mark 15:34 (RSV).

36. Rilke, *Stories of God*, pp. 126–127.

37. Samuel Beckett, *Waiting for Godot* (New York: Grove, 1956), p. 10 (act 1).

38. William Butler Yeats, *Autobiographies* (London: Macmillan, 1956), p. 106. See my discussion in *The Way of All the Earth* (New York: Macmillan, 1972; rpt. Notre Dame: University of Notre Dame Press, 1978), p. 139.

39. 1 Thessalonians 5:21 (RSV).

40. George MacDonald, *Proving the Unseen*, ed. William J. Petersen (New York: Ballantine, 1989).

41. The last words of the Buddha as quoted by Bruce Chatwin, *The Songlines* (New York: Penguin, 1987), p. 179.

42. H. G. Wells, *The Outline of History* (Garden City, N.Y.: Doubleday, 1956), p. 942.

43. Rilke, *Duino Elegies*, trans. Edward Snow (New York: North Point, 2000), p. 5.

44. Ibid., p. 9.

45. Ibid., p. 51.

46. Rudolf Otto, *The Idea of the Holy*, trans. J. H. Milford (London: Oxford University Press, 1923).

47. Tolkien, *Lord of the Rings*, p. 190.

48. Heinrich von Kleist, "On the Marionette Theatre," trans. Idris Parry in *Essays on Dolls* (London: Syrens/Penguin, 1994), p. 3. See my discussion in *The Mystic Road of Love*, p. 100 and pp. 107–109.

49. These dances and this song cycle are in the appendix of my *Road of the Heart's Desire*.

50. Rilke, *Duino Elegies*, p. 41.

51. See my discussion of this saying of Heraclitus in my *Reasons of the Heart*, p. 92.

52. Rilke, *Duino Elegies*, p. 51.

"God is spirit"

1. John 4:24 (RSV).

2. Tolkien, *Lord of the Rings*, p. 1122.

3. From the Sarum Missal as quoted in *The Oxford Minidictionary of Quotations* (Oxford: Oxford University Press, 1983), pp. 4–5. I found it in *The Sarum Office Book* (Salisbury: Brown, 1914), p. 144:

> God be in my hede
>   and in myn understandynge,
> God be in myn eyen
>   and in my lokynge,
> God be in my mouth
>   and in my spekynge,
> God be in my herte
>   and in my thynkynge,
> God be at myn ende
>   and at my departynge.

4. Hegel in the Preface to his *Phenomenology of Spirit*, trans. A.V. Miller (Oxford: Oxford University Press, 1977), p. 14.

5. Patricia McKillip, *Riddle Master* (New York: Ace, 1999), p. 179.

6. Elie Wiesel, *The Trial of God* (New York: Random House, 1979), pp. 63–64. See my discussion in *The Homing Spirit*, pp. 74–75.

7. Shakespeare, *King Lear*, act 1, scene 1, line 293 in *The Pelican Shakespeare*, p. 1068.

8. See my discussion in *The Mystic Road of Love*, p. 24. The three sentences from *Don Quixote* are quoted at the end of that book in my song "The Thinking Heart" on p. 132.

9. Arthur Zajonc, *Catching the Light* (New York and Oxford: Oxford University Press, 1993).

10. Franz Cumont, *After Life in Roman Paganism* (New Haven, Conn.: Yale University Press, 1922) and *Lux Perpetua* (Paris: P. Guethner, 1949).

11. Nicolas Malebranche, *Oeuvres*, ed. Genevieve Rodis-Lewis and Germain Malbreil (Paris: Gallimard, 1979), vol. 1, p. 1132 (my translation). See my discussion in *Love's Mind*, pp. 86–87 and in *Reading the Gospel*, pp. 7ff., and pp. 9f. on Simone Weil.

12. Saint Augustine, *Confessions* (Chadwick), p. 209 (bk. 10, chap. 34).

13. Isak Dinesen, *Last Tales*, p. 26.

14. Diogenes' description of Plato's philosophy in *Herakleitos and Diogenes*, trans. Guy Davenport (San Francisco: Grey Fox, 1983), p. 47 (aphorism #47).

15. Saint Augustine, *Confessions* (J. J. O'Donnell), vol. 1, p. 101 (bk. 8, chap. 12), *tolle lege, tolle lege*.

16. Tolkien, *Lord of the Rings*, p. 266.

17. Heidegger, *Discourse on Thinking*, p. 85.

18. Tolkien, *Lord of the Rings*, p. 540.

19. Ibid., p. 957.

20. Wittgenstein, *Tractatus Logico-Philosophicus* (Ogden), p. 107 (##6.44, 6.45, and 6.522).

21. Heidegger, *Concept of Time*, p. 12E and p. 13E.

22. Ibid., p. 22E quoted above in "The Riddle of Eternal Life" note 1.

23. Jerzy Kosinski, *Being There* (New York: Grove, 1999).

24. Tolkien, *Lord of the Rings*, p. 1100.

25. See my discussion of these lines written in the breviary of Saint Teresa of Avila in my *Homing Spirit*, p. 80. My translation here is slightly different.

26. Kierkegaard, *The Concept of Dread*, trans. Walter Lowrie (Princeton, N.J.: Princeton University Press, 1957), p. 139 (title of the last chapter).

27. Heidegger, *Concept of Time*, p. 12E and p. 11E.

28. Kierkegaard, *Concept of Dread*, p. 142.

29. Tolkien, *Lord of the Rings*, p. 982.

30. Heidegger, *Concept of Time*, pp. 1E to 2E, quoted above in "The Riddle of Eternal Life," at note 35.

31. E. M. Forster, *Howard's End* (New York: Knopf, 1946), p. 214 (chap. 22).

32. Wittgenstein, *Tractatus Logico-Philosophicus* (Ogden), p. 106 (#6.43).

33. Etty Hillesum, *An Interrupted Life*, trans. Arno Pomerans (New York: Pantheon, 1983), p. 169.

34. John Ruskin, *Modern Painters*, vol. 3 (London: George Allen, 1897), p. 165.

35. My translation of "Tout le malheur des hommes vient d'une chose, qui est de ne savoir pas demeurer en repos dans une chambre" in Pascal, *Pensees* #139 (ed. Brunchivicg) in *Oeuvres Completes* (Paris: Editions du Seuil, 1963), p. 516.

36. Kafka, *The Great Wall of China*, trans. Willa and Edwin Muir (New York: Schocken, 1974), p. 184 (#104). See my discussion in *The Homing Spirit*, p. 70.

37. Goethe, *Faust,* part 1, Gretchen am Spinnrad, translation of

Meine Ruh' ist hin,
Mein Herz ist schwer

in *Oxford Minidictionary of Quotations*, p. 178.

38. Maxim Gorky, *Reminiscences of Leo Nikolaevich Tolstoy,* trans. S. S. Koteliansky and Leonard Woolf (New York: Huebsch, 1920), pp. 12–13. See my discussion in *The Homing Spirit*, p. 73.

39. Tolstoy, "The Kreutzer Sonata" in *The Portable Tolstoy,* ed. John Bagley (New York: Penguin, 1978), p. 538.

40. Saint Augustine, *Confessions* (Chadwick), p. 201 (bk. 10, chap. 27).

41. See my discussion of "God is enough for me" in *The House of Wisdom*, pp. 35–36.

42. Meister Eckhart, *Parisian Questions and Prologues*, trans. Armand A. Maurer (Toronto: Pontifical Institute of Medieval Studies, 1974), pp. 85–86. See my discussion in *The House of Wisdom*, pp. 3–4.

43. John 6:63 (RSV).

44. 1 Peter 3:11 (KJ).

The Practice of the Presence

1. Patricia McKillip, *Riddle Master*, p. 179. M. Louise Haskins quoted by King George VI in a Christmas broadcast in 1939 (quoted above in "A Vision Quest," at note 26).

2. Wittgenstein, *Tractatus Logico-Philosophicus* (Ogden), p. 108 (#7).

3. Ibid., p. 53 (#4.1212).

4. Heidegger, *Discourse on Thinking*, p. 55.

5. *Brihadaranyaka Upanishad*, II, 4 as trans. by Juan Mascaro, *The Upanishads* (Baltimore: Penguin, 1965), pp. 132 and 45. See my discussion in *The Way of All the Earth*, pp. 193 and 228.

6. My essay on matter as a dimension is at the end of my book *The Mystic Road of Love*, pp. 137–141, note 59.

7. Wittgenstein, *Tractatus* (Ogden), p. 103 (#6.36111).

8. Ibid., pp. 106–107 (##6.4312 and 6.432).

9. Max Jacob, *The Dice Cup*, p. 5.

10. Kant, *Critique of Pure Reason*, trans. F. Max Muller (New York: Doubleday, 1961), p. 471. See my discussion in *City of the Gods*, p. 217.

11. John 17:3 (RSV).

12. McKillip, *Riddle Master*, p. 75.

13. On "wandering joy" in Meister Eckhart see Reiner Schurmann, *Meister Eckhart* (Bloomington: Indiana University Press, 1978), p. xiv. See my discussion in *The Homing Spirit*, p. 71 and Meister Eckhart on "the wayless way" quoted in Bruce Chatwin, *The Songlines*, p. 179 (on the same page the last words of Buddha, "Walk on!").

14. *Conversations of Goethe with Eckermann*, ed. J. K. Moorhead, trans. John Oxenford, intro. Havelock Ellis (New York: Da Capo, 1998), p. 324 (conversation on April 10, 1829).

15. Franz Kafka, *Tagebücher* (New York: Schocken, 1949), p. 475 on May 4, 1915 (my translation). See my discussion in *Reasons of the Heart*, p. 5.

16. See my discussion of this principle in *Reasons of the Heart*, pp. 56–63.

17. Meister Eckhart quoted by David Applebaum in the epigraph of his book *The Vision of Kant* (Rockport, Mass.: Element, 1995).

18. Meister Eckhart quoted above in note 13. See my discussion in *The Mystic Road of Love*, p. 119 and in *Reading the Gospel*, p. 37.

19. See my discussion of the transcendence of longing, taking the phrase from Theodore Adorno, in my *Peace of the Present*, p. 73.

20. See my discussion of this saying of Pascal in my *Reasons of the Heart*, p. xii.

21. Theodore Adorno, *Kierkegaard*, trans. Robert Hullot-Kentor (Minneapolis: University of Minnesota Press, 1989), p. 140.

22. See my discussion of this saying of Pascal in my *Reasons of the Heart*, p. 144.

23. Psalm 46:10 (RSV).

24. McKillip, *Riddle Master*, p. 175.

25. Meister Eckhart quoted by Heidegger, "The Pathway," trans. Thomas F. O'Meara in *Listening* (Dubuque, Ia.: Aquinas Institute, Spring 1967), p. 7. See my discussion in *Mystic Road of Love*, p. 61.

26. Chatwin, *The Songlines*, pp. 175–176.

27. Gerard Manley Hopkins, "The Starlight Night" in *Hopkins: Poems and Prose* (New York: Knopf, 1995), p. 24. See his "Author's Preface" on rhythm, ibid., pp. 117–122, and his "Poetry and Verse" on inscape, ibid., pp. 123–125.

28. Tolkien, *Lord of the Rings*, p. 162.

29. I quoted this with my former student Heather Hue's permission in *The Music of Time*, pp. 74–75.

Index of Names

JOHN S. DUNNE

is the John A. O'Brien Professor of Theology at
the University of Notre Dame and the author of nineteen books,
including *The Road of the Heart's Desire: An Essay on the Cycles
of Story and Song* and *A Journey with God in Time: A Spiritual
Quest,* also published by the University of Notre Dame Press.